# New Mexico
# SCOUNDRELS

# New Mexico SCOUNDRELS

## Outlaws, Rogues & Blatantly Wicked Men

Donna Blake Birchell

THE
History
PRESS

Published by The History Press
Charleston, SC
www.historypress.com

First published 2024

Manufactured in the United States

ISBN 9781467157124

Library of Congress Control Number: 2024935305

*For Howard Bryan, an extraordinary New Mexico historian, author and columnist, without whose thorough research and dedication most the characters in this book would have been lost to history.*
*I tip my hat to your legacy and hope to do it justice.*

# CONTENTS

# ACKNOWLEDGEMENTS

To Samantha Villa, who started this journey and gave me encouragement to continue. Thank you!

To those who have been held captive while I drone on about history and still love me—namely my family, Jerry, Michael and Justin; your unwavering support is the reason I'm still partially sane. And no, I probably won't stop buying books! Much love and deep gratitude to you all!

To Carol and Richard Estes, whose enthusiasm for my books warms my heart and keeps me going. Thank you for your constant friendship; it means the world to me. Carol, it's been great to be able to get back to our road trips again! Richard, thank you also for always being on the lookout for great research material.

To the unstoppable John LeMay, I thank you for your expertise, your guidance, your "pep talk" abilities and, most importantly, your friendship. Thank you for helping me keep it simple!

Without the support of you, dear readers, this would all for naught. Thank you for taking an interest in the scribbles of a history buff.

# INTRODUCTION

*If a man has friends enough, he can disappear without too much trouble.*
—*C.L. Sonnichsen*

From the beginning of time, there have been scoundrels in history. Sometimes fueled by greed, mental illness, a complete loss of conscience or all the above, people grew more brazen the farther west they traveled in the new land. Anonymity was a huge draw to this wild land. Before the invention of the telegraph in 1832 and the final installation of the first transcontinental telegraph system in 1861, a person could commit a crime in one town and move to an adjoining town thirty miles away; the news would not arrive for many weeks, giving the criminal time to plan and execute another attack.

With more than 77,861 million acres of land in the Land of Enchantment, there was a great opportunity for bandits to hide. Many hid in plain sight, while others had a sequence of cleverly disguised hideouts they utilized as they traveled throughout the countryside. Sometimes called Robber's Roosts, the hideouts provided a haven for the gang to relax, regroup and plan in relative safety. There are many known hideouts scattered throughout New Mexico and probably as many unknown. Of course, with these came stories of buried treasure, but those tales are for another book.

In what would be known to the world as the New Mexico Territory after 1850, these ruffians could not have dreamed up a better location for their get-rich-quick schemes and reigns of terror. This formidable landscape included mountain ranges, barren deserts, vast grasslands and deep canyons, all scattered throughout the 121,697 square miles of rangeland under turquoise skies. Every section of the territory has resources unique to the area and therefore attracts unsavory elements who are attempting to hide out or start a new life.

## Silver and Gold

Gold fever hit the New Mexico Territory hard in the 1820s—way before the California Gold Rush in the 1840s. Although California exceeded our gold volume by leaps and bounds, the New Mexico Territory proved to be gold-rich lands as well. The Land of Enchantment is littered with old mine sites, tunnels and mining ghost towns, which speaks to the amount of the precious metals taken from the hills. Towns such as Golden, Elizabethtown, Los Cerrillos, Lake Valley, Kingston and Hillsboro, just to name a few, were once bustling settlements that sprang up to support the growing miner populations.

Populations exploded, expanding a meager tent city into a full-fledged town of more than three thousand souls, nearly overnight. To the gamblers, shady ladies and con men, these were prime picking grounds, so the unscrupulous were sure to follow. Brothels, saloons and gambling houses were usually the center of the towns until families began to venture farther west.

## Well-Known Bad Men

After the Civil War, refugees became the prey, so they fled west to a land of promise and possible opportunity. Unfortunately, many of the bad men crept in as well and took advantage of the lawmen being overwhelmed by the increasing populations. Many of the more well-known of these desperados made the New Mexico Territory their stomping grounds, lending a hand to the escalating chaos. Texas transplants were some of the most influential in shaping the outlaw history of the New Mexico Territory.

We will touch lightly on a well-known character so we can give more attention to some of the lesser-known individuals, who in some cases were every bit as dangerous as Butch Cassidy, Doc Holliday or Clay Allison; all wandered the vast lands of this territory.

Lake Valley housed the Bridal Chamber, an extraordinarily rich silver mine, with 2.5 million ounces being produced from 1881 to 1893. *Courtesy of author*.

# BILLY THE KID

If you live in or anywhere near New Mexico, you have heard of Henry McCarty, alias Henry Antrim, alias William H. Bonney, alias Billy the Kid. The Kid was a presence in nearly every part of the state in his lifetime. This is a big deal especially since during his lifetime, he was hardly recognized and thought to be a nuisance more than anything else.

The world of Billy the Kid has expanded globally, with people from all corners of the world interested in the young outlaw. Outlaws are alluring. They bring excitement to our lives—possibly since they were able to do some of the things we may have secretly wanted to do. Maybe not the crimes so much, but to have the freedom, the fearlessness and respect that followed many of the more well-known Old West characters, which makes it hard to remember that the lives these people led were filled with hardships, danger and, most times, early death. But most importantly, the victims of these characters should be remembered as well—most of them had the bad luck of being in the wrong place at the wrong time and were 90 percent innocent. They were tragically taken from this world on the crazed whim of a drunken or callous outlaw. Real life in the western United States during this era was never as glamorous as the movies have tried to portray.

Much controversy surrounds the short life of the boy outlaw. Many heated debates have arisen just from whether he was killed by Sheriff Pat Garrett or allowed to live and start a new life elsewhere. We will not add to this debate in this book. So much has been written about the exploits of Billy the Kid, New Mexico's most famous outlaw—literally hundreds of books, articles and Internet posts—that we would not possibly be able to add anything new. We will leave Billy to the scholars.

Most of the events covered in this book are gleaned from the articles written in the

As the most famous outlaw of New Mexico, Billy the Kid is still a hotly debated subject in some historical circles. *Courtesy author's collection.*

early newspapers of the region and are focused on certain events. As with most media, you must take some with a grain of salt and consider the era in which these characters lived. Writing styles varied from paper to paper—some were cut-and-dried with no sympathy for the criminal, while others romanticized the exploits, lifting them up to be folk heroes. Also, political correctness did not exist in the Old West.

So, sit back, grab your favorite beverage and be prepared to drink in the incredible exploits and fantastic tales of these schemers, dreamers and downright dangerous people who formed New Mexico.

# MEANEST OF THE MEAN

## VICENTE SILVA AND HIS FORTY BANDITS/ SOCIETY OF BANDITS

Mob violence was one of the most terrifying forms of intimidation and control widely used in the Old West. In Las Vegas, New Mexico, which is often described as the "wildest of the wild," one of the worst outlaw gangs ruled the region with an iron fist. Las Vegas was described by Carlos C. De Baca in his pamphlet about the town: "The town of Las Vegas had been taken over by murderers, thieves and prostitutes, their drunken brawls were the order of the day at all hours. The barking of .45 guns were almost as common to the ear then as the honking of auto horns are in our present day....No peaceful person of sane mind dared to step into the unlighted, unpaved street after sunset." One of the worst of the gangs was known by many names—the White Caps, the Silva Gang, Vicente Silva and His Forty Thieves and the Society of Bandits were the most common. One of the most accurate was Monsters of Perversion.

As the purported owner of the Imperial Saloon on the Plaza in Las Vegas, Vicente Silva could easily recruit his clients, who might owe him a favor. The Santa Fe Trail literally passed in front of his establishment, providing thirsty travelers with a promise of a cool place in which to have a drink. Vicente was known to have a house on Moreno Street, directly behind the saloon, so it was an easy commute to work for him and his family. Rumors of tunnels, branching out from under the Moreno residence to the saloon

Renaissance Revival home at 225 Moreno Street in Las Vegas, said to have been owned by White Caps member Vicente Silva. *Courtesy of author.*

and other locations, were said to have been used by "respectable townsmen" who wanted to partake in the entertainment also provided on the Imperial upper floors.

Starting out as a bartender, Silva, who hailed from Bernalillo County, New Mexico, was born in 1845 and was reared around the Native tribes, where it was said he witnessed many murders and robberies. By 1877, he and a dozen vaqueros had gone to Wyoming for a year. There he met the wife of a Mexican railroad laborer, and they left for Colorado together. The body of the woman's husband, Felipe Aguilar, was found months later near Cheyenne. The head had nearly been cut off, and there were other mortal wounds as well. While in Colorado, Silva is thought to have found a small silver mine and used the monies gained from this to open his saloon in Las Vegas. The Imperial Saloon featured a big mahogany bar with beautifully appointed gambling rooms located upstairs.

Sharing his newfound wealth with the community and orphanages, Silva thought that he had bought the trust and loyalty of the town, but when reports of secret meetings began to surface, Silva's paranoia went into overdrive—he trusted no one. His operations began to be attacked, and cattle as well as sheep were being stolen by the hundreds. The death of a young rancher, George Payson, was blamed on the gang, as he was a prime target for theft. Many hides of Payson's cattle were found on Silva's ranch. Tales of bodies buried under the floor of the Imperial also circulated.

According to the *Albuquerque Morning Journal*, "His victims were always native people, usually freighters, who came in from the country supplied with money." Plots were discovered against Silva and his gang, so the outlaw took cover in Taos—taking his young adoptive daughter, Emma, with him and leaving his wife alone in Las Vegas to face the angry mobs if necessary. Taos proved to be too dangerous as well since it was close to the scenes of his crimes, so he fled to Coyote, a small village in the mountains near Los Alamos.

Vicente Silva, who sported a red beard, was the most feared overlord of Las Vegas and San Miguel County; no one, not even his own family, was safe from his increasing wrath. As an extremely jealous and paranoid man, Silva was dangerous. This fact was especially true since he was also under the influence of his young, temperamental mistress, who was said to have been envious of Silva's wife. With Vicente's complete attention, the mistress was able to convince the man that his family might be plotting to turn him in to the vigilantes, even though this gang was a mafia-like organization and terrorized the entire region around Las Vegas, New Mexico.

Patricio Maes was an unfortunate victim of the Silva Gang after being lured/forced to the Imperial for a drink and meeting. Silva was told that Maes was about to reveal all of Silva's operations to the authorities. A mock trial was staged in which Maes was found guilty. He was found the next morning hanging from the bridge over Gallinas Creek, which divided the two parts of Las Vegas. His death occurred during a blinding snowstorm on October 22, 1892. His stiff, snow-covered body was a shocking sight for the citizens the next morning. The coroner's jury decided that Maes had been lynched for an unknown crime. Although Silva and his gang were suspected of this crime, no one dared mention the accusations.

Silva also accused his brother-in-law, Gabriel Sandoval, who was a part-time bartender in the Imperial, of an incestuous affair with his sister, who was Silva's wife, Telesfora. No matter the protests of innocence, the hired goons, some of them law enforcement, killed the man on January 23, 1893, and dumped his body unceremoniously into an old cistern. Silva's wife was beside herself in trying to find her brother, constantly questioning her husband about Sandoval's whereabouts. Annoying Silva to no end.

It had been Silva's hope to garner enough money from the robbery of the William Frank Mercantile store in Los Alamos to escape to

Imperial Saloon was the planning site of the death of Patrick Maes, set into motion by Vicente Silva and his forty thieves. *Courtesy of author.*

Mexico with his mistress and adopted daughter, Emma. There was just one problem: his wife. In a plan said to be devised by Silva's mistress, a letter to lure his wife purportedly from her brother, Gabriel, explained that he and her daughter were safe at Silva's Coyote home. Vicente then commissioned two of his thugs to help remove his biggest irritation. The ruse worked, as a worried Mrs. Silva was picked up in Las Vegas by her husband's men and taken to Coyote to see her family. Silva had his wife under constant surveillance to try to catch her with another man, to give a good reason for his upcoming actions, but when that plan failed, he resorted to more drastic measures.

A fight between the couple broke out, as Telesfora Silva was not accepting Vicente's answers to her questions. Then Vicente drew a large butcher knife and plunged it into his wife's chest, killing her instantly; she was just thirty years old. Silva and his men carried the woman's body to an arroyo located about a quarter mile from the village of Coyote and threw her in. The arroyo bank was then pushed over just enough to cover the body, but Telesfora's feet were still visible.

As the men walked back to the house, the question of payment was addressed, and it was decided that the payment was not adequate for the job performed. Since there is no honor among thieves, Silva was shot point-blank in the head by his own man with a .45-caliber pistol, robbed and put into the same arroyo as his wife—with the feet showing. According to reports, even the cutthroats thought that Silva killing his own wife went too far.

Vicente and Telesfora were found by a passing cowboy who saw the skeletal remains of feet peeking out of the sand of the arroyo near Coyote, New Mexico, two years after their deaths. The man who was said to have taken Silva's life, Antonio Jose Valdez, would later become a peace officer for the village of Wagon Mound.

On May 19, 1893, the *Las Vegas Daily Optic*, unaware of Silva's death, ran a list of notices for wanted criminals and their crimes. Silva was mentioned in this list and was most likely responsible for all the unsolved crimes registered with the police station but was wanted for only two indictments for stealing, for which Governor William Taylor Thornton was offering a $200 reward for his arrest. This notice was published in the newspapers a bit late, for on that day Silva finally met his just reward, after the tyrant had fled to the small community of Coyote near Los Alamos, where he had another home, taking with him his adopted daughter, Emma.

Emma Silva's story was a tragic one as well. The local tale said that a baby girl was found in an abandoned stable building known as John Minner's Stables on the west side of Las Vegas on March 5, 1885; her parentage was never discovered. Rumors stated she belonged to a prominent couple from the east side of the town or a woman of high society who left town shortly before the child was found, but nothing was proven. The child was then placed under the guardianship of Vicente Silva. This makes one wonder if the girl was indeed Silva's daughter by his mistress, placed so she would be found and he could play the hero. It is odd that a child would be placed with a man with such a horrible reputation. What better way to exact revenge on your wife than to have her raise your mistress's child?

Silva was a doting "father," and Emma never had to want for anything. Sent to convent school in Taos, the young girl had no idea what a monster her adoptive father was until after his death. Said to be "beautiful and…[with] evidence of good blood and natural culture," Emma was taken to Missouri by some Americans, who befriended her after her family's deaths. As the sole heir to the Silva empire, Emma was placed under the guardianship of George Varela, of Clay County, Missouri, and would receive small payments from the estate. Records show that Emma returned to Las Vegas to marry

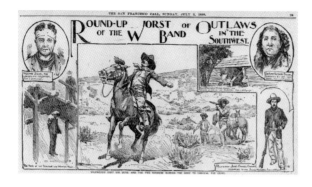

Vicente Silva's gang exploits were chronicled in an article in the *San Francisco Call* on Sunday, July 3, 1898. *Courtesy author's collection.*

Victor Rodriguez in 1903 or 1904 in the Old Town Catholic Church at the age of eighteen while a search for her true parents was ongoing. According to Howard Bryan in an article written in 1961, Emma's tragic story did not end there: "In 1911, her clothes caught fire as she was standing by an open fireplace at her home is Las Colonias. She suffered severe burns and died eleven days later."

The members of the Silva Gang, who were thought to be among the first to organize crime in New Mexico, did not fare well either, as many served time in the state penitentiary and several were hanged. The group disbanded after Silva's death. The last surviving member of the gang died in 1940 in Guadalupe County. The better-known gang members were Richard Romero, called "The Roman," who served as Silva's first lieutenant; Guadalupe Caballero, El Lechusa ("The Owl"), who was a spy, personal aide and lieutenant; Juan de Dios and Tomas Lucero, who were twins and were known cattle rustlers; Sostenes Lucero, who was Tomas's son and specialized in cattle rustling and murder; Martin Gonzales y Blea, called "The Moor," who was part Native and an excellent horseman and tracker; Manuel Gonzales y Baca, alias El Mellado ("The Dull One"), who was a puppet for Silva; Dionicio Sisneros, alias El Candelas ("The Icicles"), who served as cook and servant for the Los Alamos house; Jose F. Montoya, alias Piedra Lumbre ("Hot Rock"), who was a stonemason but liked to drink and was said to have sold his soul for Silva's whiskey; Antonio Jose Valdez, alias Patas de Mico ("Pussyfoot"), who walked with a half trot/half tippy-toe gate (he was deadly too, as he was Vicente's slayer); Zenon Maes; German (Herman) Maestas; Manuel Maldonado; Hilario Mares; Jose Chavez y Chavez; Eugenio Alarid; and Julian Trujillo.

The actions of this brutal gang of men left an everlasting, indelible mark on the community of Las Vegas, New Mexico, and are still discussed today.

# HOODOO BROWN GANG:
# SIX-GUN SYNDICATE/DODGE CITY GANG

Hyman G. Neill—part-time lawman, part-time gunman, full-time bad man—reportedly received his nickname of "Hoodoo Brown" from a dance hall girl in Las Vegas, New Mexico, where he was the leader of the Dodge City Gang, which was also sometimes known as the Six-Gun Syndicate. A mystery arose when Hoodoo Brown was buried under the name Henry G. Neill by his family. An undertaker's misspelling? Possibly.

Mr. Neill could fit into several categories in this tome, as he dabbled in both sides of the law but found the criminal side to be more lucrative. Serving as the justice of the peace also served Neill's pals well, as they were able to be above the law on nearly every occasion. His exploits were well documented in the local newspapers from the fall of 1879 upon his arrival through the spring of 1880. Declaring himself mayor and justice of the peace of the tributary, Neill began what was described as a "dictatorship" over the community. A police force was developed, mainly from Neill's friends from Dodge City, Kansas, many of whom would be considered to have stood on the other side of the law. The justice doled out by Hoodoo Brown generally saw any friend or associate of his who found himself in his court to be released, while any others would do their jail time.

The May 1, 1965 edition of the *Southwesterner* touted, "Hoodoo Brown and his Six-Gun Syndicate were too tough even for Billy the Kid." Neill, described as a tall, slender man with a pencil-thin mustache over his even thinner lips, gave off a debonair presence in his plaid suit topped with a slightly cocked derby hat. Although Neill may have been unassuming, his friends were not—this crooked, wannabe lawman was backed by names like Dave Rudabaugh, Mysterious Dave Mather, Wyatt Earp, Joe Carson and Doc Holliday. Rudabaugh and Mather were appointed to the police force as soon as Neill became justice of the peace.

Since Las Vegas did not have a mayor, judge or city council, Neill was in charge and began to call himself "Squire Neill." Rumors began to fly that this presumptuous man was actually Hoodoo Brown of Dodge City and that his "friends" were part of the Dodge City Gang, whose reputation had them as "the worst collection of cutthroats in the West." These rumors were proven true by the gang's actions quick enough. Rudabaugh, Carson and Mather were suspected of robbing the stagecoaches and trains that came into Las Vegas—Hoodoo's plan to get more money. Brown's main objective was to get as rich as possible.

Other than those already mentioned, Hoodoo's friends included Joshua J. Webb, who was a cowboy from Kansas who turned lawman and who found himself on the wrong end of the law when he was involved in a brutal gunfight in the Bill Goodlett Saloon, where Wyoming rancher Michael Kelliher was shot and killed by Webb on March 2, 1880. Hoodoo immediately declared Webb innocent of all wrongdoing. Unfortunately for Webb and Hoodoo, the grand jury was in session at this time in Las Vegas. During the hearing, evidence was brought forth that stated Brown had selected Kelliher as a "clay pigeon" for one of his officers to take out since the rancher had been displaying a large amount of cash around town from the recent sale of his ranch and was bragging about his athletic abilities.

The grand jury quickly made its decision for indictments against Webb for murder and Brown for larceny. Brown was also the acting coroner, so any of the possessions the victim had on his body were transferred to Brown's pocket. This included $1,950, out of which the funeral expenses were extracted, but the rest was returned to Brown's pocket when he absconded from the scene, some say, with the widow of City Marshal Joe Carson, who was killed in the Close and Patterson's dance hall on January 22, 1880, by three men who were later hanged, as she was seen leaving Las Vegas on a train destined for Houston, Texas, with Joe's body in tow. Kansas newspapers reported that Brown stepped off the train in Parsons, Kansas, and was joined there two days later by Joe Carson's widow; their meeting was said to be of an affectionate manner. "Neill, the widow and the coffin have been skylarking through some of the interior towns of Kansas ever since." It is unclear whether Joe Carson was buried in Houston or not given the previous sentence and why Mrs. Carson would be carrying the casket around with her. Hoodoo Brown would not return to New Mexico after this time, leaving his friend J.J. Webb with the potential of paying the ultimate price for his actions.

Joshua J. Webb was the scapegoat for the Kelliher murder since he had bungled the plan set out by Hoodoo and made everything too obvious. Webb resigned the next day, stating that police work did not pay enough. With Hoodoo gone, there was no one to fix the situation, even with the testimonies of Dave Mather and Sport Boyle for his defense. On April 9, 1880, Webb was sentenced to hang by Judge Bradford L. Prince. The execution was set for February 25, 1881, which would not happen. Governor Lew Wallace (of *Ben-Hur* fame) commuted Webb's sentence to life in prison in March 1881.

Webb was not actually a bad man, having careers such as teamster, miner, cattleman, buffalo hunter, trader and saloonkeeper; he was just caught up in a bad group. It was his gunfighting skills that would get him into the trouble

A three-story windmill in Las Vegas plaza had a dual purpose: water source and gallows. *Courtesy of Palace of the Governors, NMHM/DCA, 014386.*

he found. Before coming to New Mexico in 1867, Webb rode in a posse with a legendary man named W.B. "Bat" Masterson. After opening the Lady Gay Saloon in Dodge City, Kansas, Webb was hired as a gunman for the Santa Fe Railway in its fight against the Denver and Rio Grande Railroad for possession of the Royal Gorge in Colorado. From this job, Webb would return to Dodge City before coming to Las Vegas to become a special detective for the Adams Express Company.

Dave Rudabaugh, a fellow law enforcement officer turned outlaw who once rode with Billy the Kid, did not like the idea of his friend spending his life in prison or possibly being hanged; he killed the jailer and threw Webb the keys, but to protest his innocence, Webb refused to leave his cell. Dave Rudabaugh was caught and imprisoned for the death of the jailer in the same jail as Webb. On December 2, 1881, Webb, Rudabaugh and five other prisoners escaped the Las Vegas jail by cutting a hole through the stone (possibly adobe) jail walls. Neither men would return to Las Vegas again.

Las Vegas did not calm down completely after the Dodge City Gang was wiped out, but it may have gotten a bit safer. The saying around Las Vegas in the era was, "This town wouldn't be so dangerous, if it didn't have all these lawmen."

## John Kinney Gang

The small village of Rincon along the lazy Rio Grande was the headquarters for one of the most dangerous outlaw gangs in New Mexico: the John Kinney Gang (or also known as the Rio Grande Posse or The Boys), a band of cattle rustlers, robbers and cutthroats who were afraid of no one. Members of the U.S. Cavalry often fell victim to the gang's acts of terrorism. Their leader, Massachusetts-born John Kinney, was often referred to by the *Santa Fe New Mexican* as the "King of the Rustlers"; he was a Civil War veteran, having joined the war in 1865, just before it concluded.

Today, the Mesilla Valley is famous for being the Chile Capital of the World, where delectable green chiles are grown to be roasted in August, giving the entire region an aroma that New Mexicans know and love. So well loved is the scent that roasted chile became the "Official Aroma of New Mexico" in 2023.

In the sleepy farming village of Rincon, John Kinney was king, a cattle rustler extraordinaire. The *Las Cruces Sun-News* wrote a tongue-in-cheek commentary about a story in the *Las Vegas Optic* concerning Mr. Kinney's departure after the cavalry showed up:

> *I see that the Optic has a correspondent here who, when under the influence of "high spirits," writes all sorts of trash and foolish nonsense. He says, for instance, John Kinney is not afraid, and is the most unconcerned man in Rincon. That beats all, for gall and check! Why, Kinney was so terribly afraid, and so treacherous, that he jumped the county and left his late comrades to be pursued by bloodhounds like gallant Major Fountain and his troops. Not afraid! Well, I would like to know why he left, then; and why he slept on the hill every night while in our town.*

Kinney was sometimes compared to Billy the Kid for his demeanor, as well as the fact several members of his gang—Jesse Evans; Charles Ray, alias Pony Deal (Diehl); and Jim McDaniels—were also involved with Billy's early exploits. In 1876, Kinney and these gentlemen were involved in a brawl with several members of the 8th Cavalry (Buffalo Soldiers) at a *baile*, or dance, near Las Cruces, where Kinney and his men received a bad beating by the soldiers.

While the soldiers were celebrating their victory, the gang was not through yet. Every window and door were covered by a member of the gang, and according to the *Southwesterner* in 1962, when "the smoke cleared away, three soldiers and one Mexican were either dead or fatally wounded." According to records, no warrants were issued for this event, but the *Mesilla Independent*

*Left*: The official state aroma for New Mexico is the roasted green chile, and Hatch is the Chile Capital of the World. *Courtesy of author.*

*Below*: The adobe walls of Fort Selden are slowly melting into the earth from which they were made. Preservation is a race against time. *Courtesy of author.*

issued "a blunt editorial warning that the twelve members of an organized band of horse and cattle thieves were known and would be brought to justice; if room could not be found in the county jail, twelve ropes and twelve cottonwood trees would be supplied." These remarks angered The Boys (led by Kinney) to the point that Albert J. Fountain was calling for the militia to be brought in to protect the town of Mesilla in Doña Ana County and himself personally since he had received a blatant death threat that he would be killed on sight.

By the time the militia arrived, the gang had scattered from Doña Ana County to go on a cattle/horse stealing rampage in nearby Lincoln County. When Kinney returned to his ranch, he found that his favorite horse had been shot and another had been stolen. Kinney suspected Sheriff Ysabel Barela, and he responded by shooting Barela in the jaw, which proved to be fatal.

Kinney left the Las Cruces area to move to Silver City, where he recruited twenty men, including Jim McDaniels and Jesse Evans, and later moved to El Paso, Texas, to recruit fifty more; they became a dangerous part of the Salt War as hired guns. Kinney and his "army" were pursued closely by members of the military and the Texas Rangers, who, it appeared, wanted revenge more than keeping the peace. The fighters crossed the border into Mexico, where Kinney injured his shoulder when he was thrown from his horse.

After the Salt War ended, Kinney stayed in El Paso, where he ran the Exchange Saloon, which served as headquarters for many New Mexico outlaws and ruffians. In an 1878 assassination attempt by an outlaw known only as "Buckskin Joe," John Kinney was wounded in his left hand. It is said that Kinney committed multiple murders and found himself "wanted" in Texas.

When the Lincoln County War erupted, Kinney arrived and rode in support of the Murphy-Dolan-Riley faction against Billy and the Regulators. Although most of his gang members disappeared into history or joined Selman's Scouts, Kinney was arrested in 1883 for cattle rustling and spent three years in Leavenworth at the Kansas State Penitentiary for his five-year conviction before being paroled in 1886. Once released from prison, Kinney did not return to his outlaw ways, but rather served in Cuba in the U.S. Army again during the Spanish-American War in 1898; then he returned to Kingman, Arizona, to work at a feedlot, living out the rest of his days as a successful miner in Chaparral Gulch in Arizona. John Kinney passed away from natural causes in Prescott, Arizona, at the age of seventy-one or seventy-two on August 25, 1919.

# BLACK-JACK KETCHUM GANG

Thomas Edward Ketchum was a handsome man who set the standards high for rugged good looks for the western outlaw, standing six feet tall with dark brown hair and a mustache. Along with his brother Sam, the two dashing men were common sights in the small mining towns that dotted the Sangre de Cristo Mountains in southern Colorado and northern New Mexico Territory. Although it is reported that Tom Ketchum was not a drinker, he did like to dance with the ladies, who were attracted to him like a moth to a flame.

Arriving in the New Mexico Territory from Texas, the Ketchum brothers were known to be excellent cowboys and worked hard with little compensation for the likes of cattle baron John S. Chisum near modern-day Roswell in the Pecos River Valley. But soon the cowboy life lost its luster, and the lure of quick, easy money was too tempting for the Ketchum brothers, who saw this land as a great opportunity waiting for the picking. The Ketchum brothers were the epitome of "too smart for their own good."

In the fall of 1896, a small band of stagecoach and train robbers emerged onto the scene in southwestern New Mexico and southeastern Arizona. This gang became known as the Black-Jack Gang, and this is where a great confusion began. Who was the true "Black-Jack"?

In 1895, an Oklahoma man, Will Christian, and his brother were

Thomas "Black-Jack" Ketchum and his brother Sam came from a wealthy cattle family before they started robbing trains. *Courtesy author's collection.*

known as the Black-Jack Gang and by some reports came to the New Mexico Territory to stir up trouble. As horse thieves and train robbers, the Black-Jack Gang were known as dangerous men. It is said that Will Christian was killed by lawmen in Clifton, Arizona, on April 28, 1897, and according to legend, this is when Tom Ketchum took over the name "Black-Jack." The moniker was passed on to the next outlaw who dared to take it on.

As Howard Bryan stated in his "Off the Beaten Path" article for the *Albuquerque Tribune* in July 1958, his research indicated that Black-Jack Christian "never operated in New Mexico or Arizona, and that the activities attributed to the mysterious 'Black Jack Christian' were actually those of Tom

Ketchum—the one and only Black Jack." His reasoning stems from court records that indicate the Christian brothers were involved in gun battles in the Oklahoma Territory in 1895 and were in prison at the time of the events for which they were blamed.

One example was told in the August 25, 1899 edition of the *Las Vegas Daily Optic*, which reported that the Black-Jack Gang began with a store robbery in Kingman, Arizona, in August 1896, where one man was killed. An attempted bank robbery in Nogales, Arizona, was foiled when a teller began shooting. From there, "they took to the mountains and escaped. Nearly a dozen men have been killed and something like $200,000 has been secured by the gang. Three times the Colorado & Southern Railroad has been held up and once the Santa Fe California Limited." These actions resulted in a $10,000 reward being placed on Tom Ketchum, dead or alive—in addition to others put up by the Wells Fargo Express Company and the Colorado & Southern Railroad. It is not certain whether these crimes were perpetrated by Tom Ketchum's gang or Will Christian's Black-Jack Gang.

In fact, Tom Ketchum was not referred to as "Black-Jack" until his capture. Brother Sam began this when he was arrested in 1899 and proclaimed to be the "brother of Tom Ketchum, the original Black Jack." Sam would later change his story before his death, noting that the "real Black-Jack" had been killed in 1897, so the controversy on who was the true Black-Jack continued.

The *Pecos Valley Argus* ran a story on May 7, 1897, that stated, "The desperado killed by Deputy U.S. Marshal Fred Higgins near Clifton, Arizona…turns out to be the notorious 'Black Jack.'" The article continued, "The real name of 'Black Jack' was Thomas Ketchum, a notorious Texas bandit, guilty of many crimes and a couple of murders." This article was the beginning of the controversy that is still being debated today.

One thing for certain is that there was a train robbery on the night of August 16, 1899, three miles south of Folsom, New Mexico. During the action, Tom Ketchum's right arm was severely injured by a shotgun blast from conductor Frank Harrington's weapon. Harrington suffered a great fate, as he was killed during the robbery—thought to be by Tom Ketchum's rifle. After Tom's capture, on an embankment, extremely weak due to loss of blood, on the morning of the seventeenth, he was transported north to a Trinidad, Colorado hospital, where he gave the name George Stevens. While in the hospital, a photograph was taken of the wounded man, from which his identity was discovered.

Another member of Ketchum's gang, William McGinnis, aka Elzy Lay, was captured in Carlsbad, located in the southeastern part of New Mexico, by Sheriff M. Cicero Stewart of Eddy County. When the special officer for the Colorado & Southern Railroad, W.H. Reno, arrived to collect McGinnis, he brought with him the photograph of George Stevens. Sheriff Stewart was able to properly identify the man as Tom Ketchum since he had worked as a cowboy with him a few years before. Stewart stated that Tom and Sam were good cowboys, quiet and not troublemakers; he was surprised to learn that they were the brothers who had committed the train robbery. Tom's identity was also confirmed by his elder brother, Berry, a wealthy San Angelo, Texas cattleman who had bankrolled his younger brothers in their own cattle business and had traveled to Santa Fe to make an authentication. He was reported to have been extremely disappointed and embarrassed by the men's actions and refused to bail Tom out, but he later paid for the defense.

Tom acknowledged to U.S. Marshal Creighton Foraker that he was the outlaw known as "Black-Jack" while in the penitentiary, but it was said he later told a newspaper reporter that he had admitted only because newspapers had blamed everything the "real Black-Jack" did on him anyway, so he might as well confess. He went on to say that the real Black-Jack was not still alive, so it could not be him. Foraker remained convinced that Tom Ketchum was indeed the "original Black Jack." Newspapers speculated that the first Black-Jack was an outlaw named Will Anderson and that after his death, the moniker was passed down to the next gang leader.

While in prison, Ketchum's gunshot wound led to the amputation of his arm by the penitentiary physician. At first refusing the operation, Tom Ketchum finally relented when he was told that it was the only way to save his life. This action sent the outlaw into depression. On August 22, 1899, authorities reported that Ketchum asked a deputy for a gun so he could shoot himself; when this request was denied, it was discovered later that night that Ketchum had attempted to strangle himself with his bandage by tying one end around his neck and the other end around his foot. It was thought that he was trying to choke himself by tightening the noose with his foot. When this did not work, he tried to swallow pins from his bandage. Surprisingly, he survived and was said to have become more talkative and cheerful afterward.

During his time of incarceration, Tom Ketchum reportedly wrote a three-hundred-page autobiography, relating all the stories of his short career as a train robber. It is extremely unfortunate that this manuscript has never been found, if it even existed at all. The outlaw claimed that he was the brains behind the heists but never participated in the execution of the plans. The shattered arm full of buckshot would beg to differ.

Ketchum's hanging was a big event at the Union County Courthouse on April 26, 1901. Picnics and children's games were planned. *Courtesy author's collection.*

Tom Ketchum was sentenced to death after he regained his health, but this sentence was halted by Governor Miguel Otero to give the outlaw a chance to have his case heard by the U.S. Supreme Court. Ketchum's attorney for this case was the Honorable Thomas B. Catron (of Santa Fe Ring fame), after he received a $1,000 retainer from Berry Ketchum for his brother's defense. Unfortunately, for the outlaw, it was all for naught.

The *Albuquerque Journal* ran a story, titled "A Terror of New Mexico," by a New Yorker named Edfrid A. Bingham on December 13, 1903, about the execution of Thomas E. "Black-Jack" Ketchum. "'Black Jack' Tom Ketchum

A gruesome scene was about to unfold before the spectators' eyes. Those closest were reportedly splattered with blood. *Courtesy author's collection.*

was a handsome man—the best-looking outlaw, they say, that ever terrorized the territory of New Mexico." After he languished in the penitentiary for two years after his arrest, Tom Ketchum's time had run out, but he was a celebrity prisoner of sorts by the end, with photographs and interviews often being taken by newspapers throughout the country.

On April 26, 1901, at 8:00 a.m., Tom Ketchum was scheduled to be hanged. The night before, the rope was tested with a two-hundred-pound sandbag at the gallows, situated on the front lawn of the Union County Courthouse in Clayton, New Mexico. As he ascended the stairs, Ketchum was heard saying, "Dig my grave deep, boys." When he reached the landing, he tested the trapdoor with his foot and asked for a hood. His request was granted, but it had to be removed briefly to place the noose around his neck.

Impatient, Ketchum reportedly said, "Let her go boys, I want to be in Hell for supper," but most likely he said, "Hurry up, boys, get this over with." With this request, the sheriff cut the trigger rope, and Ketchum quickly fell, with ghastly results. His head was sheared off completely. Ketchum's body landed squarely on his feet and stood for a moment before collapsing. Blood from the decapitation flowed freely as the large audience, which included children, gasped in horror.

Several factors were blamed in the botched execution. It was said that no one in Clayton had experience in hanging; that Ketchum had gained a considerable amount of weight while in jail, as the ladies of the town kept him fed quite well; and that the rope was too long or stretched during testing. All these factors contributed to Tom Ketchum taking his gruesome place in history.

After his death, his head was sewn back on, and Ketchum was buried in the middle of the Clayton Cemetery; apparently, neither the Catholics nor the Protestants wanted him included in their midst. A lone tree is the grave's only companion, and the grounds and jail of the Union County Courthouse are said to still be visited by Ketchum's ghost.

## Stockton Gang

### *Porter Stockton*

The *Weekly New Mexican* dated March 28, 1881, stated of Porter Stockton's arrival in Rio Arriba County, "Porter Stockton, running away from Animas, Colorado, arrived in our midst. His previous record was a terrible one, and his course in Animas City, only confirmed all that had once been said about him. The launching at once amongst us of a desperado of the worst-kind was probably the worst thing that could have happened." Porter and Ike Stockton were products of both the Colfax and Lincoln County Wars by 1878 and were driven out of those counties, but they started to congregate in the far northwestern county of San Juan, where they were attempting to become the overlords of the farming communities there.

The article went on to say that Rio Arriba County was poorly mismanaged and run by only the rich elite, causing "no point of law and order enforced." The newspaper was fearful of the situation in the county, likening it to be "worse than the Lincoln County War due to the lawlessness in the region." Stockton was a "terror" to any community in which he resided, so the claims seemed to fit nicely. He claimed to have taken the lives of nineteen men, but the paper speculated that it could have been closer to thirty in his lifetime.

Stockton's murder history is a long one. His first kill was when he was but twelve years of age, when a man allegedly called him a liar. Porter was then credited with killing Antonio Arcibic (most likely Archibeque), a Mexican man in Cimarron, for snoring in 1876, seeing this as the only way to get the man to stop. He was arrested for this murder in Colorado by Sheriff Rinehart and returned to New Mexico for trial. Attorneys for Stockton included Frank Springer and Melvin W. Mills, who were hotshot lawyers in those days and members of the Santa Fe Ring. While in the Cimarron jail, his brother, Ike, was kind enough to bring him some pie around September 13, 1876. When the jailer opened the cell for Ike, he was rewarded with a pistol across the back of his head. Porter and the jailer exchanged places, and Porter escaped on the waiting horse, complete with a Winchester rifle.

Stockton rode north to the village of Otero, where he was again arrested by the marshal, Hurricane Bill. Once again managing to escape the jail, Porter rode through the streets of Otero looking for his jailer. Spying a man who looked like Hurricane Bill, Porter opened fire without verifying, adding another life to his tally. While in Animas City, Stockton beat a Black barber nearly to death for not giving him a close enough shave; he then fired his pistol at the man, grazing his scalp. The *Santa Fe New Mexican* claims that he last murdered Den Gannon, a horse thief.

Porter Stockton was reported by this paper to have jumped the claim of a man who drowned in Animas. He then was accused of wounding the man who transported the man's widow to town to make her rightful claim. This injury resulted in the man's death. Stockton was also accused of committing murder at a local dance in Rio Arriba County. Despite his crimes, Porter was allowed to continue his spree. "He continually and repeatedly breathed forth his threats of death to numerous persons living in the community, until people were paralyzed with fear."

By June 1881, the Stockton Gang was partnering with the Charles Allison Gang and split up to do double the damage in Rio Arriba County. Vendettas were waged against local ranchers who had brought charges against the gang for cattle theft.

When the citizens finally stood up against Stockton, his wife, in defending her husband, was wounded in the event. In the October 3, 1881 edition of the *Weekly New Mexican*, it was reported that after the deaths of Porter and Ike Stockton, the property values in Rio Arriba County rose at least 25 percent. "How much Rio Arriba County has been injured by Stockton and his gang there is no telling, but now that the country is rid of them the riddance can be better appreciated. The days of ruffianism in New Mexico are fast drawing to close, and the fact is a good thing for the Territory." After the brothers' deaths, their gang still committed several robberies before filtering out of history.

# SMALL-TIME OPERATORS

## Mesa Hawks Gang

The Mesa Hawks Gang received their rather romantic name from two sources. One was the area where the gang could most likely be found—at the top of a mesa, to get a bird's-eye view of the open landscape of the eastern New Mexico plains; the other was derived from the leader Henry Hawkins's last name.

Activities for the gang were recorded by the newspapers from 1888 to 1912. Henry Hawkins was born in Platte County, Missouri, in 1861 and went to work for the Fowler Packing Company in Kansas City, Missouri, as a youth. After getting into some trouble in Missouri, Hawkins decided to move west and became one of the "bad citizens of the New Mexico Territory."

The fledgling gang's claim to fame stemmed from an incident in Fort Sumner, New Mexico (the site of Billy the Kid's grave), in 1902. On January 27, 1902, the Mesa Hawks decided that the post office in the remote village was easy pickings. While holding up the Pecos Mercantile Company Store, a teenager by the name of Felipe Beaubien was gunned down when he attempted to flee. Felipe was said to be a foster child of the Beaubien family.

One of the lesser members of the gang, George George Massagee, told a story that states the posse was already pursuing them from an earlier robbery and had fired on them, to no injury. Massagee claims that it was Hawkins who chose the site of the next job, and he was forced to join in on the crime. The plan included the gang members entering the store in pairs,

Fort Sumner, a town made famous as the death site of Billy the Kid, is also the location for a deadly robbery. *Courtesy author's collection.*

with Massagee being the odd man out—so he was assigned to watch the street and hold the horses.

Hawkins and Potter entered the store first, ordering the occupants to throw up their hands. When one person was slow in following the order, Hawkins allegedly struck him on the head with his pistol, leaving a deep gash. Massagee stated that he heard a gunshot from inside the store and assumed that it was when Beaubien was killed. The outlaw remained outside for what he described as an hour before entering to help with loading the spoils, and then the gang rode away quietly and stopped at an adobe structure around twelve miles from Fort Sumner to count the money.

Among the items taken were United States mail, ammunition (which they dumped in a stream as they left), a small amount of personal property and enough money to split with the gang so that they all received eleven dollars each. Certainly not worth a life.

Members of the gang included George Cook, George R. Massagee, John W. Smith (alias Sam Bass), Whit Neal, Robert "Black Bob" McManus (alias Ed Franks/Frank Potter), Joe Roberts and, of course, Henry Hawkins. After the tragedy in Fort Sumner, most of the gang escaped to Arizona, pursued by the Arizona Rangers. George Massagee was captured by the Mescalero Agency on the Mescalero Apache Reservation near modern-day Ruidoso about a week after the event and was given five years in the territorial penitentiary by a jury. Due to the similarities of the names, early newspapers often confused George Massagee with another outlaw of the time, George Musgrave.

John W. Smith (alias Sam Bass) was the third outlaw to be discovered, in the Arizona Territory, and was also given five years in the territorial penitentiary in Santa Fe for his involvement in the crime. Robert "Black Bob" McManus, who claimed to be a cattle inspector, was found near Raton. McManus created a ruckus when law enforcement tried to establish his real name. First he was arrested by Sheriff Farr in Trinidad, Colorado, as G.W Franks and claimed to be the last surviving member of the Black-Jack Ketchum Gang; then he was later identified by federal officers as Frank Potter, a member of the Mesa Hawks. No matter his real name, he remained jailed in Raton as officials tried to find witnesses who could prove the man's identity.

Whit Neal was found at his girlfriend's cabin in the northern Arizona Territory near the town of Clifton. The *Tucson Citizen* reported that Neal was taken into federal custody without incident, although he had a Winchester at the ready, "showing that he was ready for business at a moment's notice, but he was given no notice at all and was compelled to leave his 'bride' in bed and surrender." George Cook and Joe Roberts were apprehended in the same area.

All three men were taken to Solomonville, Arizona. Released into federal custody, the three outlaws were returned to New Mexico. Along the way, Joe Roberts was able to escape his captors and slipped away, never to be seen again. In 1936, a skeleton of a man, a shotgun and a dead horse were found in the hills near Glendale, Arizona. The Arizona Rangers strongly suspected that these remains belonged to Joe Roberts.

According to one account, each of the gang members denied shooting the young man, but it still did not stop Neal and Cook from receiving life sentences. Rosamond Greer, Henry Hawkins's wife, stated in court in an unrelated case that she was told by Bill Cook that her husband was dead. Greer obtained a divorce and remarried a local rancher by the

Sheriff Pat Garrett was responsible for orchestrating the massive irrigation project in the Pecos Valley before his death. *Courtesy author's collection.*

name of John Madden. According to newspaper accounts, Henry Hawkins was never heard from again.

Local lore states that legendary sheriff Pat Garrett got into a gun battle with Henry Hawkins at a water tank in central New Mexico. Close to running out of ammunition, Garrett negotiated a truce with Hawkins, to which he also agreed. The outlaw escaped again and was never captured.

# OUTLAW LAWMEN

## Dave Kemp

In the tiny hamlet of Eddy, New Mexico (soon to be known as Carlsbad), brothers Charles Bishop and John Arthur Eddy from Colorado Springs, Colorado, dabbled in the cow industry and recognized an immense opportunity in the region as they set up their cattle operations near the Pecos River. Soon the vision Charles Eddy had for the southeastern part of the New Mexico Territory came to fruition, and the tent city became a fledgling town in need of law enforcement.

Due to Charles Eddy being a teetotaler, alcohol was not allowed within the townsite, and any violation of the bylaws would result in the relinquishment of land and property back to the Town Company, headed by the Eddy brothers. Eddy envisioned the ultimate town in his mind, modeled after Colorado Springs, but the town soon grew so quickly that the rules were changed just as fast.

Medicinal alcohol was being consumed by the barrelful, as people were allowed to write their own prescriptions. Something had to be done to stop the lawlessness. Enter Dave Kemp, who at age seventeen was convicted of murder when he came to the aid of a friend, resulting in a death; he was sentenced to twenty-five years in a Texas prison. It has been written that Kemp, not accepting this sentence as his fate, became a model prisoner and prevented a jailbreak, which shortened his sentence. Others state that Dave was *part* of the prison break, as he jumped off a second-story balcony and broke his ankle.

At age thirty-three, Dave Kemp was elected sheriff of Eddy County by one vote. According to the *Las Vegas Daily Optic*, on November 13, 1890, "Dave Kemp voted for his opponent C.H. Slaughter, for sheriff of Eddy County. This bit of political courtesy made the vote a tie. If he had cast his vote for himself, he would have been elected by two votes." Once he was elected, the *Pecos Valley Argus* declared on December 27, 1890, "Now that Dave Kemp has been elected sheriff, it is to be hoped that he will quit chewing gum, which is the only bad habit he has. He is perhaps the only sheriff-elect in New Mexico who does not use tobacco, drink liquor or indulge in profanity." This is an odd statement, since Kemp was part owner of the Lone Wolf, a tent city saloon built directly on the road leading to the construction site of the irrigation flume, and would later be part owner of the Silver King Saloon two miles away from Eddy in a den of sin called Phenix, where he was also the law. Dave Kemp, Tom Fennessey (gunslinger) and Ed Lyell, a local brothel owner, would become powerful forces and feared men in this "town of poison."

The local newspapers seemed to have a love affair with Dave Kemp for many years, as the Texan could do no wrong for his three years as Eddy's first sheriff. This was until February 17, 1897, when he was accused of killing James Leslie "Les" Dow, a political rival, as he was leaving the post office. Dow had just been elected as Eddy's third sheriff on January 1 and was looking forward to a long career. According to the *Carlsbad Current Argus*, "a feud of some sore was said to have existed between Dow and Kemp." That was putting it mildly.

Many have stated that the reason for the rivalry was the result of Dow beating Kemp for sheriff, but that was not true, as John Walker was elected the second sheriff. The stories spread by Dow may have led to some mistrust among the townsfolk, who stated, "The saloon owners eventually hired their own law to try and keep the peace, men like Dave Kemp and Walker Bush, who many believed were worse criminals than the ones they arrested, pistol-whipped or shot. Phenix might be a pretty safe place for a man to visit if there were no armed officers there."

A short blurb in the *Eddy County Citizen* in July 1892, by the citizens of Hope, New Mexico, a town about fifty miles northwest of Eddy, pretty much sums up the distrust in the actions of their elected official, who seemed to rule with the end of a pistol: "Sheriff Kemp, of Eddy is in our settlement. Next time Dave comes up we want him to send word in advance. We need time to hide out, and don't want to be scared to death."

Les Dow was said to be a more dangerous gunman than the man who killed him, but Dave Kemp had the element of surprise.
*Courtesy author's collection.*

Behind the scenes, Kemp had a few shady deals going on and hired his gunslinger half brother, Walker W. Bush, as chief deputy to help him "keep the peace." Les Dow owned a saloon in the village of Seven Rivers, fifteen miles north of Eddy, and was a known gunslinger himself, but what caused the strife stemmed from Dow's days as a cattle brand inspector, even though Dow was one of the citizens responsible for recruiting Dave Kemp to service in Eddy in 1890.

With no love lost between the men, Dow accused Kemp of cattle rustling and had him arrested. This came as quite a shock to the town that their sainted sheriff, whose only known vice was chewing gum, could be accused of such a crime. Kemp was acquitted, much to the town's relief, but Dow was still not happy; the men began taking accusatory swings at each other. Kemp, not to be outdone, accused Dow of the same charge, but the charges did not stick. Discontent and corruption ruled Eddy County.

Les Dow was shot in the jaw that fateful day outside the post office, lingering all day and night in excruciating pain. Kemp was arrested, and he immediately pleaded not guilty due to self-defense. In the late 1800s, a law existed that in part stated that if a dispute between two people ended in death and both were armed, it was automatically self-defense—no matter which party was killed. The trial, which was a sensation, brought in many onlookers from around the territory. Even with the dirty laundry that was exposed, David Leon Kemp was acquitted of all charges.

Seemingly unscathed by the events, Dave Kemp remained in Eddy; got married in 1888, a second time in 1898 and a third time in 1903; fathered four children (all of whom tragically passed away young); and, according to some, moved back to Texas to live with his sister. Kemp died of a heart attack on January 10, 1935, at the age of seventy-three in Booker, Lipscomb County, Texas, where he had a cattle ranch.

## Charles Perry/William "Bill" Cook

Charles C. Perry had a flawless record as sheriff and ex-officio collector of Chaves County until 1896, when he was removed by Governor Thornton under suspicion of embezzlement. Funds thought to have been taken included $2,798.71 from the Territory of New Mexico, $4,413.17 from Chaves County, $1,703.47 from the Chaves County school districts and $48.65 from the City of Roswell. The sum of these funds equaled $9,144.00—a total very close to the monies owed to him for the capture of the Oklahoma outlaw Bill Cook the previous year but which were never paid by the Southern Pacific Railroad or Wells Fargo Bank. It cost Perry more than $10,000 of his own money to complete the arrest and transport—all with anticipation of being reimbursed.

Perry eventually paid back $1,200 of the outstanding amount to the county when required, but spent seven months away from New Mexico in Dallas/Fort Worth, Texas, and other centers for the railroads to collect the reward money still owed him. Rumors stated that Perry, who captured Bill Cook on the Farrel Ranch near Fort Sumner, embezzled the money and went to South Africa to hide out, although the Fort Worth account seems more likely. There were even rumors that Perry had joined up with the Black-Jack Ketchum Gang and participated in a train robbery near Grants, New Mexico, in 1897. This was never proven.

Bill Cook was described in the *Santa Fe New Mexican* in 1895 as the "most noted desperado, train robber and murderer in the United States." The newspaper went on to say that Cook was "backed by a horde of blood-thirsty ruffians armed to the teeth." Some news sources stated that Cook had an army of more than one hundred rough men ready to follow him to the death—it was closer to fifteen. The depiction of Cook's appearance did not match the *Santa Fe New Mexican*'s terrifying portrayal. In truth, Cook was between twenty-one and twenty-two years of age, about five feet, eight inches tall, weighed about 165 pounds and had dark hair and gray eyes.

Running from a train robbery in Texas, Cook stopped to rest his horse near the Yates corral at the Farrel Ranch in Lincoln County, New Mexico, five miles from Fort Sumner. He had been in the territory for only ten days before Sheriff Perry and Deputy Tom Love of Borden County, Texas, happened upon the outlaw, who was not armed at the time of discovery. The arrest was easy for the lawmen but would prove to be costly for both groups. Cook was said to be "very cool under pressure" but was disgusted by being

The current Chaves
County Courthouse,
built in the Beaux-
Arts style, ushered in
a new era when it was
completed in 1890.
*Courtesy of author.*

captured. The famous outlaw was a novelty, and as he was being transported by train to Santa Fe in the smoking car, curious onlookers gathered around to get a glimpse of the shackled train robber.

Cook was quoted as saying, "Wonder if these damn fools think I'm a wild animal." The *Albuquerque Journal* reported that the crowd dogged the outlaw so much that the young man was seen to shed a tear. Coming from a tough family and raised in the equally tough Indian Territory of Oklahoma, that seems doubtful. His brother George was also an outlaw and received life imprisonment for the attempted robbery of a post office in southern New Mexico in 1907. His other brother Jim was also a train robber and was buried at the Roswell, New Mexico cemetery after he died from tuberculosis, which he contracted in the Roswell jail while being incarcerated for his crimes.

He was first transported to Santa Fe for safekeeping at the penitentiary and then was moved to Fort Smith, Arkansas, to face trial, where it was said that Cook and Henry Starr were cellmates and played cards together. Cook was eventually sentenced in April 1895 to forty-five years in the Albany, New York penitentiary and was assigned to make shirts in the prison.

After turning Cook over to the Fort Smith authorities, Perry fully expected to be paid for his troubles, but unfortunately, he was not paid a cent in reward money. Although it was not proven that the missing Chaves County funds were taken by Perry, his reputation was irreparably damaged, and he would continue to be known as the "disgraced sheriff." The embezzlement charges were eventually dismissed by the Chaves County District Court in 1899, but the damage was already done.

## Milton Yarberry

As New Mexico's largest city, Albuquerque has been known to have a violent history. When the railroad entered the picture in 1880, it attracted more than a few rough characters into the growing town. Murder, robbery and vagrancy were commonplace, clarifying the need for law enforcement. Enter Milton J. Yarberry as the first constable for Precinct 12 for the Bernalillo County settlement in February 1881.

For a lawman, Yarberry had a checkered past. Reportedly, Milton was born around 1850 in Walnut Ridge, Arkansas, and by the time he arrived in New Albuquerque, he had been involved in "shootings in both Texas and Colorado, and he was a suspect in a slaying in Las Vegas, New Mexico," according to Howard Bryan in his article in the *Albuquerque Tribune* dated February 8, 1973. Thought to have ridden with the ruthless outlaw Dave Rudabaugh, a pal of Billy the Kid, Yarberry was suspected of killing a man in Fort Smith, Arkansas, while robbing the man's home.

He was described as a tall, stoop-shouldered man with gray eyes and a black moustache, and reports also indicate that the newly elected constable was illiterate: "Naturally a man of less than ordinary intelligence, Yarberry's education has not tended to improve the work of nature, as every mean instinct of his narrow brain has been fostered and nursed from childhood." He was not well liked by the citizens because he "carried things with a high hand" and had a reputation as a trigger-happy bully.

The black marks were adding up for the lawman quickly in New Albuquerque, but everything came to a head on March 27, 1881, when Yarberry shot and killed twenty-four-year-old Henry A. Brown in front of the Girard Restaurant on the corner of Second and Railroad Avenues (now known as Central Avenue). Brown was a messenger for the Adams Express Company and the son of former Tennessee governor Neill S. Brown. The dispute stemmed from jealousy. Apparently, young Henry was eating dinner with Yarberry's love interest, Sadie Preston, the widow of Yarberry's business partner turned saloon girl and bunco artist, after the pair had shared a buggy ride along Railroad Avenue.

Angry words were exchanged, resulting in Yarberry shooting Brown in the chest, possibly twice, which resulted in his death on a Sunday afternoon in March 1882. Milton turned himself into his friend Sheriff Perfecto Armijo, claiming that it was a case of self-defense, although it was believed that Brown was unarmed. This plea resulted in an acquittal, and Yarberry was able to return to his duties as town marshal.

By June, Yarberry was in another fracas that also resulted in death as he and a friend were walking along Railroad Avenue drinking whiskey. The pair heard a gunshot and investigated, asking a group of men who fired the shot. They pointed at a man walking on the other side of the street. Milton shot the man without asking any questions, killing him instantly. Witnesses reported that the trigger-happy marshal did a "jig" around the dead man, stating, "I've downed the son-of-a-b----!" Unfortunately for Yarberry, the man he "downed" was Charles D. Campbell, an unarmed railroad carpenter, who was known to have never owned a weapon. Milton's luck with the self-defense plea finally ran out, as he was tried, convicted and sentenced to death by hanging after a three-day trial.

In the months prior to his death, Yarberry, claiming his innocence, escaped custody of the jail in Santa Fe with three other convicts on September 9, 1882, only to be captured again on September 12 by Santa Fe police chief Frank Chavez and his posse. When he was found, a newspaper reporter told Milton that he looked pale, to which he was reported to have replied, "Maybe. But I ain't sick, and I ain't scared either."

Although he was not well liked in Albuquerque, Yarberry's death was quite unconventional. A new type of gallows was used that, unlike the normal image of hangings, jerked the convicted upward instead of dropping them through a trapdoor. It is thought the phrase "jerked to Jesus" was coined using this barbaric mechanism.

On February 9, 1883, Milton Yarberry was led to the gallows by Sheriff Armijo in front of 1,500 spectators to answer for his crimes, all the while proclaiming, "Gentlemen, you are hanging an innocent man." According to the *Santa Fe Daily New Mexican* and the *Albuquerque Morning Journal*, his was not an easy death. As the mechanism jerked Yarberry upward, his head violently struck a crossbeam. It is not completely known if the catastrophic jerk from the noose or the impact of his head on the wooden beam was the true means of death; nevertheless, Milton Yarberry's death would be the last one using this type of gallows in New Mexico. It is rumored that Yarberry was buried at Albuquerque's Santa Barbara Cemetery with the noose still around his neck; to add insult to severe injury, his name was misspelled on his headstone, which has since been either stolen or lost.

How many lives did Yarberry take during his lifetime? Historians seem to waver on this quite a lot. Three seems to be the magic number, although Yarberry never paid for two of these, claiming self-defense. How many lost their lives to John Armstrong (a name many claim to be Yarberry's alias or true identity)? This fact was confessed before his death to his friend Elwood

Maden. Yarberry relayed that he was born in 1849 in Arkansas as John Armstrong. It was as Armstrong that he committed his first killing—this was the reason he changed his name to move west in 1873, so the exact number is not widely known.

From 1873 to 1875, the newly minted Yarberry ran with some dangerous men, namely Dave Rudabaugh and Dave Mather, and took part in several robberies with them. After these men parted ways, Yarberry joined the Texas Rangers as a part of Company B of the Frontier Battalion, serving honorably for three years. He then became John Johnson and opened a saloon with Bob Jones, who turned on him when a bounty hunter came calling about the 1873 murder. It is said that the body of the bounty hunter was found outside Decatur, Texas, after this event.

# FAMOUS GUNFIGHTERS

## ROBERT CLAY ALLISON

The phrase "gentleman gunfighter" seems like a contradiction in terms, but it fit Robert Clay Allison perfectly. Although he committed some horrific actions during his lifetime, he was always a champion of the innocent.

Born in Tennessee in 1841, Clay, as he wanted to be called, worked his family farm until the Civil War erupted in April 1861. Although Clay was raised by a Presbyterian minister, he developed a deep hatred for anyone who hailed from the North, as well as Black people. During his first enlistment, Clay became overzealous in his desire to rid the world of Northern menaces—so much so that he threatened his commanding officers with death if they did not continue in campaigns where the Union soldiers had already surrendered.

A childhood accident that caused what today we call a traumatic brain injury was blamed, and this likely convinced the Confederate army to let the Tennessee soldier go. Clay was able to find a commander who had ideals more to his liking, enlisting again one year later with General Nathan Bedford Forrest. Serving as a spy for Forrest, Allison was captured and sentenced to be executed, but his determination and small hands allowed him to escape this fate and return to Tennessee. Some of Allison's early life and military service has been convoluted, making it difficult to know the true story.

After the war, Allison moved to Texas with his family to start a cattle business. His involvement in several murders during his time in Texas included a dispute with a neighbor over a watering hole near the Brazos River that resulted in the two men digging a hole and having a knife fight to the death—the winner was to bury the loser. Clay obviously won, but it was time to move on, as his opponent's family were furious with him. This story has been challenged by historians for years.

Northeastern New Mexico and southern Colorado held a particular soft spot in his heart, and this is where he did most of this cattle ranching. The quiet village of Cimarron, New Mexico, was never the same after Clay's arrival around 1869, as he provided the local newspapers with enough fodder to keep them afloat. If you visit the St. James Hotel in Cimarron, you will be able to see the results of Clay's desire to dance naked on the bar while discharging his weapon—just check the holes in the tin tile ceiling. During a remodel of the bar, more than four hundred bullet holes were found under the tin tiles, the majority of which were likely from Clay's pistols.

Clay was a defender of the innocent and took it upon himself to defend a cause, even without due justice. He is associated with at least two vigilante lynchings—one in defense of the family of Charles Kennedy, whose story is also included in this work, and the other in revenge for the killing of circuit minister, Reverend Franklin J. Tolby, whose death sparked more violence in the Colfax County War.

Allison was quick, unpredictable and a little crazy, so this made him the most observed gunfighter in New Mexico and Texas. He even had a run-in with Wyatt Earp in Kansas. His uncanny ability to assess a situation and predict the outcome usually led to the deaths of his opponents.

*Top*: Clay Allison was dangerously unpredictable and one of the most watched gunfighters in the West because of his volatility. *Courtesy author's collection*

*Bottom*: General Nathan Bedford Forrest was a huge influence, be it good or bad, on the young Rebel soldier named Clay Allison. *Courtesy author's collection.*

This is also the reason why Clay never received a gunshot wound, except for the one he inflicted on himself while attempting to "borrow" mules from Fort Union in what he described as a prank.

As he was a heavy drinker, Clay's moods would change with the amount of whiskey he consumed. He was said to always carry at least five gallons of whiskey with him during cattle moves, and his other love was dancing—as previously mentioned, usually naked. He would insist others dance with him, to which they were terrified to say no since Clay's pistol was usually trained on their feet.

Always a wanderer, Allison sold his northern New Mexico ranch and moved south toward the violent cow town of Seven Rivers. It was there that he became friends with the Larrimore and Jones families and spent a great deal of time in the local saloon. By the time he moved south in 1885, Clay had married America "Dora" McCulloch in Mobeetie, Texas, and become a father to Patti Dora.

On July 3, 1887, while attempting to guide a heavily loaded freight wagon across an arroyo, Clay became dislodged from the seat and ended up on the ground just as the wagon lunged forward. Clay's neck was broken from the weight of the wagon, and according to whichever account you believe, he either died at the scene or lasted for a few hours and passed away later in the day at the age of forty-five. Debates still swirl about whether Clay had been drinking that fateful day, but it was certainly not the type of death one would imagine for such a colorful character of the Old West.

Clay's pregnant wife had to bury her husband that day at a pioneer cemetery near their Pecos, Texas home. America's daughter, born seven months after her father's death, would be his namesake, Clay Pearl. Mrs. Allison remarried to a local cattle rancher and moved to the Fort Worth area, where she and her daughters enjoyed privileged lives. Miss Clay Pearl inherited her father's bad luck unfortunately and passed away in a tragic automobile accident with her granddaughter later in life.

Due to constant flooding, the occupants of the Pecos Cemetery were moved away from the sandy ground to a new cemetery that did not flood. The citizens of Pecos decided that Robert Clay Allison was special, so they gave him the distinction of being the only gunfighter to have his own cemetery, as he was buried in the middle of the town square next to a replica of Judge Roy Bean's courthouse and saloon on the grounds of the West of the Pecos Museum on August 28, 1975. Allison's headstone reads, "He never killed a man that did not need killing." He also earned the nickname the "Gentleman Gunfighter," which was placed on a second headstone.

## BUTCH CASSIDY

Reports made by Arizona resident Frank Gilpin stated Butch Cassidy and a "fellow by the name of Harry Longbaugh," aka the Sundance Kid, were working in Alma, in the Gila Region of the New Mexico Territory, as cowboys for the W.S. Ranch in the Mogollon Mountains between the years of 1898 and 1901; Captain William French was the part owner and foreman of the ranch. It was said Butch also worked as a bartender in the Morris Coates Saloon in Alma. It is said that Butch used some of the money the gang garnered from a train robbery near Folsom, New Mexico, in Alma, which piqued the suspicions of the Pinkertons, although nothing came from it.

French had just let his entire ranch crew go because he suspected them of cattle rustling. Butch, going by the name Jim Lowe, got hired by French immediately following the incident. Butch was made foreman by French, which allowed him the ability to hire on the Sundance Kid under the alias Tom Capehart. Other members of the Hole in the Wall Gang arrived at the ranch as well, and French would later find out who his best ranch hands truly were. Butch and Sundance were also known to join in the fight against cattle rustlers for the W.S. Ranch.

In William French's book *Recollections of a Western Ranchman*, the famous outlaws were remembered to be on their best behavior, with no drinking, gambling or shooting, when they reached the end of the line in Magdalena, New Mexico. As the largest shipping point and last stock highway in the United States in the 1890s, Magdalena was the place to go for a ranch outfit to kick up its heels after a long trail. The gang did not want to be recognized, and French always received compliments on his well-behaved crew.

Butch Cassidy and the rest of the gang fit right in with the rest of the cowboys. French commented, "The way Butch Cassidy handled those cattle over that long and dusty trail was a revelation. Frequently, they had to go as much as seventy-five miles without water, but he never dropped a hoof and there was no tail to his herd when they arrived at the road."

A Mr. Gilpin told the *Southwesterner* in January 1962 that he was taught to shoot by Sundance, who also told him, "There was only one good reason for a pistol and that was to shoot a man and the main thing to learn was how to fix an enemy, so he won't cause you anymore trouble." Sundance was described as a different type of man than Butch, as Cassidy was not a killer—Sundance certainly was. Said to always have a smirk on his face, Sundance would sulk around and did not hesitate to use his pistol.

LeRoy Parker (*far right*), alias Butch Cassidy, worked in the Coates Saloon in the mining town of Alma, New Mexico. *Courtesy author's collection.*

Magdalena, New Mexico, a colorful historic mining town between Socorro and the Very Large Array, was "trail's end" for local cattle. *Courtesy of author.*

Thought to be a Robin Hood character, Cassidy was said to use his "earnings" from the robberies to purchase supplies that homesteaders needed to survive—barbed wire, seed and so on. This was thought to be the reason the outlaw turned from being a cowpuncher to a train robber, as he could help more people that way. Highly respected by other men, Cassidy was said to have saved more lives than any other man in the West, according to Maude Baker Eldredge, whose family was close friends with the train robber.

Butch, Sundance, Elza Lay and George "Kid" Curry had just held up the Union Pacific Overland Flyer in Wilcox, Wyoming, on June 2, 1899, during which Sheriff Joseph Hazen was killed by Kid Curry. This event sent the gang to their Robber's Roost in western Wyoming to lay low for a while and split up the loot. The gang with Cassidy, Sundance, Kid Curry and Elza Lay then headed south into Arizona and New Mexico. It is thought that Cassidy and his gang had hideouts from Montana to New Mexico—the W.S. Ranch was used as one from 1898 to 1899 due to its proximity to the Mexican border.

The gang was back in the news in August 1900 when they blew up the Union Pacific Express car near Table Rock, Wyoming, and again in July 1901 when they relieved the Adams Express Company of $40,000 worth of bank notes after they used a tad too much dynamite and blew up the entire car.

Whether or not Butch Cassidy and the Sundance Kid died in Bolivia, as rumored, they certainly made their marks on the Land of Enchantment.

# John Henry "Doc" Holliday

Best known as Wyatt Earp's sidekick, Doc Holliday was a fixture in Las Vegas, New Mexico, for a short period of time before moving on to Tombstone, Arizona. After Earp set up a saloon on Centre Street (now known as Lincoln Avenue), Holliday was probably his best customer. Doc hung his shingle up for his dentistry office a few blocks from the saloon.

During his short stay in one of the wildest towns in the West, Doc got involved in a shooting on Centre Street in front of his saloon. A frontiersman, U.S. Fifth Cavalry veteran and scout for fourteen years by the name of Mike Gordon wandered into the saloon in July 1879 after drinking heavily for days and shortly regretted his decision. The *Las Vegas*

Doc Holliday's dentist shingle hung for a short time in the most dangerous frontier town of the Old West, Las Vegas, New Mexico. *Courtesy author's collection.*

*Optic* continually fretted about the conditions in its town, writing, "Indeed Las Vegas is a civil, law abiding but lively place. Life and limb are as safe here as anywhere on the globe; however, if you want a shooting match, just for the fun of the thing, you needn't leave town for the purpose of hunting a cowboy. You can be accommodated here."

It is said Gordon had his nose bitten off during an earlier fight by a gambler he was stealing from. One can imagine Gordon might not have had the best of attitudes toward the gambling man. The gambler may have grabbed Gordon by both ears with a "grasp of iron" and disfigured the man with his teeth. Drinking whiskey and shooting up the local dance halls were his favorite pastime, and this time he chose Doc's saloon since his girlfriend worked there. The drunken man tried to convince his girlfriend to go across the street to another saloon, but she refused. Gordon left vowing to kill somebody or be killed himself by morning. He would receive his answer moments later.

"Gordon was standing in the street to the right of the hall," reported the *Las Vegas Gazette*, "after some of his threats and drew a revolver and fired, the bullet passing through the pants legs of a Mexican and stuck in the floor in line with bartender who was standing at the rear of bar." In all, it was thought there were up to five shots fired, after which Gordon disappeared. He was found a few hours later in great pain from a gunshot wound. Gordon died after being taken to his girlfriend's room that morning. "In the afternoon the coroner held an inquest, and the jury returned a verdict of excusable homicide." Although the *Gazette* did not name Gordon's assailant, it was widely thought to have been Holliday.

Considered by the local newspaper as "a shiftless, bagged-legged character—a killer and professional cut-throat and not a whit too refined to rob stages or even steal sheep," Doc Holliday was not as well liked as Hollywood portrayed in later years.

Gordon, although a rabble-rouser, was well thought of in town, and people were genuinely upset when they heard about the killing, especially since all he was trying to do was to get his girlfriend to go across the street to another saloon. Doc was afraid for his life, thinking a vigilante group would catch up with him soon. He was arrested but "crept through one

The exact location of Holliday's grave is unknown. Glenwood Springs, Colorado, erected this cenotaph in his honor after his death at age thirty-six. *Courtesy author's collection.*

of the many legal loopholes which characterized Hoodoo Brown's judicial dispensation." Although Doc had two charges filed against him in 1879, one for "keeping a gambling table" for which he was fined twenty-five dollars, the one for killing Gordon was lowered to "carrying a deadly weapon." Nonetheless, Doc had left town by August 1879 to meet up with the Earps in Tombstone, Arizona. The rest, as they say, is history.

# THE APACHE KID

Known as Haskay-Bay-Nay-Ntay by his people, the Apache Kid was thought to have been born to the White Mountain Apache people in the middle of the Apache Wars in about 1860 on the San Carlos Reservation land near the Gila River in Arizona, which is now the beautiful Cibola National Forest in central New Mexico.

As was the custom of the time, warring factions of Native tribes would capture young people to use as slaves and in bartering. Haskay-Bay-Nay-Ntay was captured by the Yuma Indians as a child but was rescued by the U.S. Army and brought to live in an army camp, where he basically would have to fend for himself on the dirt streets. Many say that his fate led him to be sent to Pennsylvania, where he was placed in the Carlisle Indian Industrial School to be groomed on how to be "civilized." He learned to speak English and largely adopted the white man's ways.

While in Pennsylvania, the young man learned about the operations of the army and soon became a scout in the early 1880s, serving under General George Crook as a sergeant. Haskay-Bay-Nay-Ntay was a trusted member of the campaign to capture Geronimo—who, coincidentally, was his relative. No one could pronounce his name correctly, so he was dubbed the "Apache Kid" by the soldiers. The Kid was commanded by Albert Sieber, the chief of scouts from 1882 until 1886.

An unfortunate series of events changed the young man forever. In 1887, the Kid was dishonorably discharged for drinking too much at a camp party and killing a man who was involved with his mother (it is unknown if this

The Apache Kid became the subject of many dime novels, as far more fiction than truth was written about his short life. *Courtesy author's collection.*

German immigrant Albert Sieber served as chief of scouts during the Apache Wars and trained the Apache Kid before betraying him later. *Courtesy author's collection.*

involvement was consensual); his father was also murdered during a fight, and so it was left to the Apache Kid to avenge his death. With the help of his father's friends, his mission was accomplished.

While he waited to be incarcerated in the guardhouse on the reservation, a small riot broke out allowing the Apache Kid to escape, only to be captured a short time later. Albert Sieber, who was his commanding officer, was shot below the knee by the Kid during the commotion. These events led to the Apache Kid and sixteen others fleeing the army camp. The Kid sent word to General Nelson Miles that he and the others would surrender, but only if the general called off his troops. Miles agreed, and the Kid complied. A court-martial followed, and the Kid fell victim to a new law that stipulated if an Indian is found guilty of crimes, they would serve their sentences in territorial prisons instead of federal ones.

Reports state that Arizona and the army planned to retry the Kid and his companions and sentence them to territorial prisons. The Kid was indeed retried and convicted once again; he was sentenced to seven years in the notoriously treacherous Yuma Territorial Jail. En route on November 2, 1899, the wagon transport was stopped, forcing the prisoners to walk up a steep grade. When they complied, the Indians were able to overpower their captors, killing two lawmen and shooting and wounding the stage driver, Eugene Middleton.

As an expert tracker and scout, the Apache Kid was able to elude the U.S. Army for more than a decade, all while committing raids on local ranches and freight wagons in the region. Most of his fellow prisoners were either killed or captured after the escape. One story tells of one of the Natives being beheaded and the head placed on a stake at agency headquarters.

Having nothing to lose, the Apache Kid was suspected of kidnapping girls from the Apache tribes to become his wives and perpetrating attacks on anyone who got in his way. Said to have traveled deep into Mexico, the Apache Kid resurfaced in the Arizona and New Mexico Territories to continue his reign of terror on the locals. His reputation of committing murder, rape and theft earned him a $15,000 reward on his head—dead or alive.

Rumors state the Apache Kid was killed by a posse in 1894 or even later in 1899 by Mormon settlers. In an article in the *Albuquerque Citizen* that ran on December 25, 1907, a bizarre claim was made by a group from Chicago, who stated they had killed the famed Apache Kid in the Sierra Madre Mountains of California. During a camping trip to the mountains, their horses were stolen, so the group followed the tracks to an Indian camp, where they claimed they killed the residents, including the Kid. The Chicagoans boasted that they took the skull of the Apache Kid and planned to give the macabre item to Yale University for the Skull and Crossbones Society once they retrieved it in a few months. No evidence has ever been produced that a skull was recovered or gifted.

A marker located in the Cibola National Forest of central New Mexico notes the Apache Kid's grave has been located in the San Mateo Mountains since 1894. In 1980, this area was designated by Congress as the Apache Kid Wilderness; it encompasses about forty-five thousand acres of wilderness land. It is likely that no one will ever truly know the fate of Haskay-Bay-Nay-Ntay. Some say that he still roams the lands of his people.

# SUPPORTING CAST

## CLAUDE DOANE/JOSE S. BACA

Although basically unknown, Claude Doane should be on top of the list when it comes to downright bad men. Doane has left the word *scoundrel* in the dirt for a long time. He was described as "one of the most desperate and dangerous outlaws who have terrorized New Mexico cattlemen for years" by the *Las Vegas Optic* in 1906. If anyone was the poster child for "you are a product of your raising," it would be Claude Doane. In November 1896, Claude and his friends George Craig and Frank Deemer were charged by Doane's mother, Mary J. Hackett, for cattle theft. Doane refuted his mother's testimony against the group.

While working for a stockyard in Albuquerque, New Mexico, in his youth, Claude took part in a plan cooked up to skim a few healthy calves from the herds as being sickly. This way, the sick calves could be removed from the rest and taken away to nurse back to health to make way for healthy cattle. When the calves were brought to health, they were then returned the original herd in the stockyards. If a calf was born at the stockyards, it was considered in the way and given to locals along with the dead animals.

This procedure caught the eye of Doane and his friends, who decided that the calves could to go to them just as well as anyone. The problem was that the thefts were not being recorded, throwing off the stockyard records, which was noticed by agent William Matson. According to further testimony, this plan was approved by Doane's mother, who eventually turned them in when Claude refused to continue. This case was eventually dismissed.

Doane, George Craig and William Jackson were convicted of cattle stealing in another case two years later in 1898 and sentenced (two years for Craig, one year for Jackson and six months for Doane) to the territorial penitentiary. Apparently, being released early showed them how easy it was to commit this theft, starting Doane on a long road of criminal activity. He showed up in an article in the *Otero County Advertiser* in February 1901: Claude's leg was shattered by gunfire, and notorious horse thief Abel Sedillo was killed by deputies after being spied in the company of stolen horses and cattle from the Isleta Reservation. Sedillo's killing was deemed justified since he was resisting arrest.

The future actions of Doane would leave a scar on the quiet town of Gallup, New Mexico, for years to come, as in July 1905, a badly decomposed body was found twenty miles north of Gallup in a canyon near Ramah by a McKinley County sheep herder, later identified as beloved schoolteacher and Michigan native Walter Lyons, who appeared to have been killed between June 4 and June 14 of that year.

Lyons would teach school for several months of the year and then travel and wander the other time. Doane would cross his path at Concho, Arizona, where Doane was working in a local saloon for Juan Lopez. After convincing Lyons that he knew locations for some silver mines, Doane was able to lure his victim to the surrounding desert, where an apparent disagreement occurred, resulting in Lyons's death.

Doane's accomplice, Jose Sustino Baca, a sheep herder from Torrance County who assisted him in many cattle and horse thefts, had many run-ins with the law before and after Claude's incarceration. Convicted of manslaughter in 1902, Baca was arrested with Doane for horse theft and was held by $1,000 bond placed by the grand jury in 1905. The pair had rounded up a herd of horses and were about to dispose of them when they were arrested by Officers Ben Williams and Fred Fornoff, who had followed them into Taos Canyon. This arrest resulted in Doane being taken to Gallup to face murder charges after one of the longest chases in the criminal history of the state—nearly three hundred miles were covered from Lincoln County to Taos.

Baca was able to escape the Bernalillo County Jail and fled to the nearby Zuni Mountains. While on the lam, Baca married a girl from the Zuni tribe and settled down in the mountains to live a "normal" life until his capture by mounted policeman Rafael Gomez. When he was returned to jail, Baca was sentenced to five years in the territorial penitentiary by Judge Ira A. Abbott, which was the longest sentence the law provided for this offense. Baca was reminded of his previous four offenses for which the length of the sentence would depend on his behavior while in prison for the first sentence.

When taken to the territorial penitentiary on November 18, 1906, for the fifth time in his career, Baca was reported to have said, "Well, this old place looks familiar to me, but I don't expect to stay long. The Governor will pardon me." To this, Superintendent Arthur Treiford responded, "Shut up. Place him in stripes and put him to work; he looks like he needs it." Baca was certainly a habitual criminal and had carried the prison numbers 382 for horse theft in 1890, 444 in 1892 for larceny, 538 later in 1892 for burglary and larceny again and 1520 in 1902 for manslaughter. This was all before his 1905 situations with Claude Doane.

In July of the same year, ex-convict and horse thief Claude Doane was convicted after withdrawing his not guilty plea and changing it to guilty to murder in the second degree. Doane's attorney, Julius Staab, was present at the hearing. He was then sentenced to ninety-nine years in the territorial penitentiary in Santa Fe for this gruesome crime.

Another big headline in the *Albuquerque Journal* on July 13, 1905, read, "The Governor Actually Fears Abduction of Son." While in jail awaiting his transfer to Santa Fe, Doane organized a group of eight men who reportedly had grievances with Governor Otero, devising a plan of kidnapping the governor's young son, Miguel, transporting him to the wild country of the Malpais, commonly referred to as the "Valley of Fires" due to the lava flow near modern-day Carrizozo. Once there, they would hold him for ransom for thirty days, all the while placing a demand for a rumored huge sum of money from the father (which they knew would be too high for the governor to meet). The demands of the outlaws would include "money, freedom and the freedom of several convict now serving terms in the penitentiary." The plan all along was to create a sensation and trouble for the governor—Miguel's life was always in jeopardy. Luckily, the plan was thwarted, but not without some tense moments for the territorial governor.

Doane was led through the prison doors on Thanksgiving Day 1905 in heavy shackles at age thirty to begin his ninety-nine-year sentence for murder in the second degree. The *Holbrook Argus* noticed that he seemed to be in good spirits despite his conviction: "If it had not been that he wore irons, he would not have been taken for a man who was about to begin a life sentence." Doane's responded to his situation by saying, "I give you my word, I'm a victim of circumstances. I've been jobbed. I trust to God that you will have mercy on me." You may draw a different conclusion soon enough. After Doane was sentenced, Judge Ira A. Abbott imparted words of wisdom to the outlaw, to which he responded, "I thank you very much for the advice, but I don't think it will do me any good."

In 1907, the *Roswell Daily Record* reported that convicted horse thief and murder Jap Clark (another New Mexico scoundrel) alleged charges of cruelty against Doane in the territorial penitentiary, supported by an affidavit by Clarence Hamilton, who was the victim of this treatment. Doane was not known for his kindness and was known to hold a position of prominence in the jail yard—the others did what they were told without question.

Once released from the state prison, Claude Doane would not stop his criminal activities; he was later found guilty of other crimes, including the enticement of, seduction by promise to wed and rape of a fourteen- or sixteen-year-old girl in 1921, for which he received a term in the state penitentiary of not less than ten and not more than twenty years. Claiming his innocence and stating that he had the mother's permission have the girl live with him, Doane also said the girl allegedly visited him every night when he worked as a night watchman—something the girl also admitted to doing. Doane being thirty-five at the time did not garner any sympathy from the jury.

In another blub in the *Albuquerque Journal* from 1921, Doane was granted a divorce from a woman he had married in 1919 whose mother had been found dead from what was thought to be self-administered poison after the wedding. Claude and his wife lived with the victim, with whom Claude also had a close relationship. Captain Pat O'Grady investigated the death, observed several peach pits on the floor around the woman and somehow determined that the poison was taken voluntarily. The victim's sister said that the woman was jealous of the relationship between Doane and her daughter since she was in love with him as well. Surprisingly, given his past and the fact that he admitted to bringing the poison, given to him by a friend, into the home to control the mice population, Claude was not charged for this death.

The rape conviction would be his fourth term behind bars—by age forty-one, he had spent half of his life in prison. During this time, it was reported, prisoner no. 1960 (Doane) purchased thirty-eight dollars in Liberty Bonds and was praised for his efforts, although he complained about his conditions at every chance possible, even suing the prison during his stay.

After being the star of the New Mexico newspapers for so long, it is difficult to think that a man like Claude Doane would fade into the background so easily, with only a few remembering his criminal actions. Possibly he moved back to the Midwest, where he may have been born, as several Claude Doanes appear in articles from Missouri to Maine after 1922. If he was in Maine at some point, he may have worked as a carpenter, railroader or businessman. In the days before the Internet, the possibilities were endless.

Jose S. Baca appears in the newspapers again in an article in the *Albuquerque Journal* dated August 8, 1931, with the headline, "Pugnacious Attitude Gets Man $100 Fine and 30 Days in Jail." Jose S. Baca was arrested after a drunk driving charge following a motor vehicle accident. After the accident, a drunken Baca allegedly attempted to fight the man whose vehicle he had just rear ended. When police officers searched Baca's vehicle, they found five empty gallons jugs they believed had contained liquor. A person by the same name was also listed as a corporation commissioner for Bernalillo County in 1928. This is all speculation, as this may or may not be the same Jose S. Baca who caused so much havoc in the territory. Past transgressions were often forgotten in New Mexico.

## Martin M'Rose: The Polish Cowboy

As a Polish immigrant, Martin M'Rose first settled in the Polish community of St. Hedwig, Texas (near San Antonio), in the 1890s. In what would prove to be a fatal decision, Martin moved west to the New Mexico Territory to

Known as the "Polish Cowboy," Martin M'Rose had some true bad luck with his shady lady wife and gunfighter attorney. *Courtesy author's collection.*

seek his rancher's dream in the blossoming cattle industry.

Honing his skills as a cowboy, M'Rose soon became a cattle buyer and was well on his way to rival some of the large outfits in the region, making a name for himself with the upper echelon of the cattle business in and around the new town of Eddy (now known as Carlsbad), but he soon became restless with the progress and was accused of "altering" cattle brands on more than 150 steers he allegedly rustled from local herds.

Martin is one of those characters who could be considered a good bad guy. There are several conflicting sources of information on Mr. M'Rose, in both newspapers and books. Some have written that Martin was a victim of circumstance, being associated with the wrong people. His business partner, Vic Queen, was a local cowboy who had great aspirations as well but was thought to be a cattle rustler. Wrong place, wrong time. Some think it was all a setup since M'Rose served as a bank commissioner in Eddy but later was found to have been wanted for rustling in Martin County, Texas.

Then there was his wife, Helen "Beulah" Jennings, a woman running from an abusive husband in Texas who was said to have taken on the world's oldest profession to support her and her young daughter (whom she disguised as a boy) but found Martin to be an easy mark. Proof that bad things happen to those who display too much wealth. Martin and Beulah were soon married in the Silver King Saloon in Phenix, New Mexico (a rowdy town two miles south of Eddy), where she worked; the saloon was owned by Eddy sheriff Dave Kemp. This relationship would ultimately bring about the end of his life.

When Martin and Vic Queen were arrested for cattle rustling, the *Carlsbad Current Argus* of April 27, 1895, stated that they were "leaders of a gang of stock thieves who have been operating successfully in Lincoln and Eddy counties." M'Rose had sold his ranch and stock just before the arrest for a reported $8,000, which was a large sum of money in his day. Not wanting to take a chance on being hanged, both men escaped to Juárez, Mexico. Beulah, newly married and with the knowledge that Martin had taken a large sum of money from the sale with him to Mexico, employed an attorney, John Wesley Hardin. Yes, *the* John Wesley Hardin.

The *Santa Fe New Mexican* ran a story on April 10, 1895, stating that Santa Fe Railroad detective Beauregard Lee of Raton, New Mexico, had been following Beulah M'Rose in her attempts to locate her husband. He got a lucky break when he noticed Beulah boarding a train to Magdalena, Mexico, at the Mexican Central Depot at Juárez. He also boarded the train and observed the meeting between husband and wife. At their discovery, Beulah drew her pistol but was disarmed. Both were arrested and taken back to Juárez, where it was found that Beulah had $1,800 in her possession. Mrs. M'Rose was released from jail with the money, soon to take up with her hired attorney, Hardin, in an extremely cozy and familiar manner.

Hardin said that he received several notes from the Juárez officials, who more or less stated that "he would never be allowed to get Mrose [*sic*] to this side of the river [United States] and that he better make himself scarce in Juarez." Not one to back down from a threat, Hardin crossed the bridge after what the former gunslinger described as being bulldozed and subjected to "saucy" talk by Tom Fennessey and his Eddy County cohort Lightfoot.

The same newspaper article described Hardin as "a spirited man and quick tempered, consequently this little Sabbath day collision did not sit well on his good-natured stomach."

After consulting with Chief Milton about the situation in Juárez, it was decided to go to a local saloon to order drinks. As they entered the saloon, they saw Mrs. M'Rose surrounded by five of Martin's friends in a meeting as well. "To have back[ed] out of the room would have looked like a retreat, so the four friends entered, saluted and took seats," according to the reporter.

As the conversation turned to the M'Rose case, tempers began to flare between Hardin and Tom Fennessey (an Eddy County lawman and the man who hired Martin as a cowboy on the VVN Ranch, owned by Eddy founders Charles and John Eddy), resulting in Hardin slapping Fennessey across the face and pointing his weapon at the lawman's chest. Quick actions by Chief Milton prevented bloodshed, as he was able to grab Hardin's pistol in the struggle. Weapons were drawn all around the table, but at Milton's urging, they were returned to their respective holsters. Still incensed about recent events, Hardin walked over to Lightfoot and "gave him a slap in the face that could be heard for a block."

Hardin did his best to reassure M'Rose he would be released from prison soon, but he would have to wait while the attorney pleaded his case with the Mexican authorities and make sure that it would be safe for M'Rose to return to Eddy County without fear of being hanged for cattle rustling. In the meantime, he and Beulah were in no hurry to acquire M'Rose's release since they were in possession of the large sum of money—Beulah had convinced Martin to entrust it to her for attorney fees. Hardin and Beulah were fixtures in the El Paso saloons and jails. Beulah was even helping Hardin pen his autobiography (which, unfortunately, has never been found) in between their drunken rows.

Deputy U.S. Marshal George Scarborough was contacted by Martin M'Rose, who by this time was desperate to speak with his wife and had found out about the status of his money. Understandably reluctant, Martin was waiting to hear from Beulah on when it would be safe for him to come across the bridge, but rumors of Beulah and John Wesley Hardin's relationship had been circulating in Juárez, enough to make Martin more than a little suspicious and angry. It was said that Martin was wanting a showdown with the famous gunfighter, who was already reportedly responsible for forty men's deaths.

Scarborough convinced M'Rose that he could cross the bridge to speak with Beulah "unmolested." The incident occurred in the middle of the Central

Buried only feet from John Wesley Hardin, the man who was instrumental in his death, M'Rose is still overshadowed. *Courtesy author's collection.*

Juarez Bridge at midnight. A dark figure motioned to Martin from across the bridge that it was safe to cross, and as M'Rose reached the American side of the bridge, two men jumped out from a patch of sunflowers on the side of the bridge and drew on Martin, who pulled his pistol. With this, M'Rose was struck with a barrage of gunfire, hit eight times in an ambush. In some accounts, Hardin is also included in this conspiracy plot, promising to split the M'Rose reward money with the gunmen, which included John Selman.

"Boys, I think you've killed me," were the last words Martin M'Rose would ever utter.

Mrs. Beulah M'Rose and John Wesley Hardin were the only attendees at the funeral for Martin M'Rose, held at El Paso's Concordia Cemetery. Ironically, Hardin would meet death a few months later at the hands of John Selman when he refused to pay up on his promise. Martin M'Rose and John Wesley Hardin are buried within ten feet of each other. Hardin's grave is an elaborate tourist attraction, while Martin's is subdued and almost forgotten.

# CHRISTOPHER "KIT" JOY/MITCH LEE/ FRANK TAGGART/GEORGE CLEVELAND

On November 24, 1883, a train robbery between the towns of Gage and Deming, New Mexico, catapulted a group of petty bandits into infamy. This would be the first major train robbery in the New Mexico Territory.

Four cowboys who were tired of the hard work on the range devised a plan to make some good money quick. The Southern Pacific Railway was ripe pickings for Christopher "Kit" Joy, Mitch Lee, Frank Taggart and George Cleveland, who devised the plan while drinking in a Silver City saloon on November 19, 1883.

Kit Joy and Mitch Lee made their way from ranch to ranch on their way to Gage, finally settling at Eaton's Hay Camp, where the two began inquiring about the exact time the passenger express would pass by the Gage switch (it was about dusk at 5:00 p.m.) and learning that the train did not stop at the switch. To remedy this situation, a piece of the rail was removed, which would cause part of the train to derail. When this was discovered, the engineer, Theopholus C. Webster, threw the train into reverse and applied the air brakes.

As the engineer and fireman, Thomas North, were attempting to stop the train, they received incoming gunfire from north of the engine compartment. The fireman was able to escape by jumping off the south side of the train and crawling on his hands and knees to a ditch for shelter, but the engineer was not so lucky—he was found two hours later, dead from a gunshot wound to the heart. Although the engineer attempted to defend himself with a rifle, it was not enough to save his life. Webster's wife later explained during her testimony that her husband had gone to work that fateful evening armed, stating that he was tired of being held up by thugs.

The express car was ransacked. Registered letters and the safe were opened. One robber was so casual with the operation that he reportedly took time to crack and eat nuts that were inside the room using his Bowie knife. A passenger, Charles A. Gaskill of Chicago, was curious as to what was going on, so he exited the train; he was immediately robbed of $155. He was the only passenger to suffer this fate, as the others remained on the train, feverishly attempting to hide their valuables anywhere possible. Once the train was robbed of the $27,000 it was carrying, the four thieves split ways and returned to their normal way of life by working as cowhands on the local ranches.

Rewards of more than $8,000 were offered by Southern Pacific and Wells Fargo for the capture of these men. It took two months, but all the men were arrested and brought to jail in Silver City, where their fingers began pointing at Mitch Lee as the trigger man in the death of Webster. On March 10, 1884, the four train robbers; Carlos Chavez, an accused murderer; and Charles Spencer, a horse thief, overpowered the guards at the jail to escape. All six ran down the street to the Elephant Corral and obtained their getaway horses at gunpoint to race out of town toward the mining town of Piños Altos.

As a source of progression westward, the Southern Pacific Railroad was also victim to numerous train robberies along the rails. *Courtesy author's collection.*

Along the way, George Cleveland was killed by Frank Taggart, who had learned that George had been tricked by a Pinkerton investigator into telling all he knew about the train robbery, which led to more charges for the other robbers. Cleveland had not wanted to participate in the escape but was forced to ride along with Taggart, who stated, "We are going to kill you anyway, you better get up here now." Cleveland was relieved of his head by a shotgun blast only a few miles away from town.

A posse of townsmen forced the outlaws into a gun battle that led to Chavez's death and the capture of Lee, Taggart and Charles Spencer. Kit Joy was still at large and would soon be responsible for the killing of a beloved posse man, Joseph N. Lafferr. Upon hearing of Lafferr's death, the fates of Lee and Taggart were sealed, as both men were promptly hanged from the nearest tree. Spencer surrendered and was returned to jail. Despite rumors of his death, Kit Joy was found eleven days later at a ranch on the upper Gila River, his leg so severely wounded by a gunshot from a deputy that it had to be amputated just below the knee in Silver City.

According to the details of the trial featured in the November 29, 1884 edition of the *Las Cruces Sun-News*, written by a court reporter who signed off as "Swamp Fox," testimony about the robbery and murder pointed directly at the remaining accused cowboy, Kit Joy, who was convicted in Hillsboro of the second-degree murder of Theopholus C. Webster and sentenced to life imprisonment.

# JOEL FOWLER

One of the most hated men in Socorro County, New Mexico, was cattleman Joel Fowler. Why? Columnist Howard Bryan explained: "When Joel A. Fowler had a bone to pick with a man, he would sometimes corner him in a crowded saloon, ask him for a 'chaw of tobacco' then shoot him when the man obligingly reached for his hip pocket. Then the pint-sized gunman [reportedly five feet, four inches tall] would turn to the bystanders with an innocent expression on his face and ask: 'You saw him reach for a gun, didn't you?' All would agree with the killer, and Fowler would go free with another victim to his credit."

Not much is known of Fowler's early life, with some sources stating that the outlaw was born in Indiana in 1849 to cultured parents. Fowler moved to Fort Worth, Texas, in 1870 to live with his uncle and quickly married. Rumors state that his young wife was unfaithful, and Fowler ended her extra relationship by putting a bullet in her lover. This event sent him to Las Vegas, New Mexico, in 1879, one of the roughest towns in the West, where he ran a dance hall, according to F. Stanley in his book *Desperados of New Mexico*.

One of the sporting girls caught his fancy, and the gunman soon married a second time to Miss Belle La Mont in the home of the notorious Confederate spy and madam Monte Verde, whose real name was Belle Siddons, in Las Vegas. The couple made their way to Santa Fe, where, as author Leon Metz states, Fowler, under the influence of whiskey, "treed practically the entire town with a shotgun until being overpowered and transported to jail." It was after his release from this fiasco that the couple moved south to the gold mining town of White Oaks in 1880. Ironically, it was in White Oaks where Fowler would take another life—that of a drunken miner Virgil Cullom, who was shooting up the town. Cullom was one of the estimated twenty-six men Fowler found it necessary to kill during his lifetime.

One of the most hated men in Socorro County, Joel Fowler had no issues with adding more notches to his reputation. *Courtesy author's collection.*

After purchasing a cattle ranch near modern-day Socorro, New Mexico, Fowler proved himself to be quite a con man. As per local lore, another of his sneaky deceits was to sell a small herd of steers to a butcher or another rancher for cash and then send one of his hands to kill the buyer and bring the cattle back to him. Pioneers of Socorro County stated that Fowler committed this deception numerous times, racking up his body count. Stories have Fowler responsible for up to twelve deaths in the two years he lived in the county. He was known as the "human exterminator," having killed an average of three men per year.

The December 20, 1881 edition of the *Santa Fe New Mexican* stated that Joel Fowler's brand was "C.O.D.," and a good number of his cattle were missing. A notice was placed in the paper that read, "Any person found with cattle branded, C.O.D would be arrested for stealing, unless showing a bill of sale from the owner." Fowler used this as an attempt to get his neighbor Charles F. Blackinton arrested for theft. According to Fowler, he set up the neighbor's cowhands to help him escape to Mexico with his cattle. The men in Fowler's story—Jim Finley, Jim Greathouse (a friend of Billy the Kid) and Jim Conley—were agreeable and decided to turn on their employer. Fowler and his chief herder then turned on them, shooting them all.

Blackinton's story differed from Fowler's, stating that it was a setup and that Fowler was the aggressor. The neighbor swore his innocence and told a story of how he had run his horse until it dropped dead and had to walk fourteen miles into town in a driving rainstorm. Blackinton claimed that being exposed to the elements caused him to have an "attack of lung fever." The conflicting stories and Fowler's reputation led the citizens to question Fowler's innocence in this matter. The truth was that Fowler and the three men were cattle rustling together, and Fowler saw this as a great opportunity to get rid of the witnesses. Greathouse became suspicious of Fowler's dealings and had begun to question the man, which led to his and his companions' deaths at Fowler's hands.

Fowler's tendency for cruelty was well known and despised. Under the influence of alcohol, he was worse. He would enter saloons with guns blazing at the ground to make the men dance. Other times he would enjoy humiliating men by forcing them to stand on their heads in corners—at gunpoint. Fowler derived great joy from his actions, but others did not see his actions as funny. His bad reputation was catching up to him.

In the *Albuquerque Daily Democrat* dated September 19, 1883, a story ran about an encounter Fowler had with a figure from his past:

> *In the Gallinas Mountains, a cattleman named Joel Fowler started a cattle hunt with several men. After leaving the ranch he found that one of the men, called Pony, was a brother of the man named Forrest whom he had*

*killed a year before. He discharged Pony, who returned to Socorro, and with a desperado named Butcher Knife Bill, returned to the Alamo Ranch with the intention to kill Fowler.*

*As Fowler was returning from the hunt, he saw Pony and Bill at his house. They drew their revolvers, Bill firing at Fowler. Drawing a shotgun, Fowler killed Bill instantly. Pony ran behind the house, firing at Fowler five times. He then ran into the house. A man named McGee, coming up and hearing of the trouble, went to the door of the house and called Pony to come out of the house. Receiving no reply, he broke the door and looked in, then Pony shot him through the head, killing him instantly.*

*Fowler then asked Pony to come out and fight it out with him. Pony refused to do so, and Fowler set fire to the house to drive him out, when Pony shot himself through the head. The three men were buried on the spot.*

After this fight, Fowler went to Socorro to face the judge, who let him go on account of his story, as he was the only survivor. While in town, trouble was always around the corner. A man named Turk had a beef with Fowler and decided that now would be a good time to renew the argument. Fowler beat the man over the head with his pistol, causing great injury.

Shortly after this trouble, Joel Fowler sold his Alamo Ranch in 1883 for what was said to have been a sizeable amount, $50,500. Wanting to celebrate his success, Fowler brought his family into Socorro, secured a room at the Grand Central Hotel and began to paint the town red.

Joe E. Cale, a salesman, was also in town during the Fowler celebration on November 6, witnessed the cattleman up to his usual shenanigans and decided to help the citizens disarm him. Fowler then surprised the good

The Grand Central Hotel in Socorro was the primary hotel in 1883, and it was said that "anyone who was anyone" stayed there. *Courtesy author's collection.*

Samaritan by plunging a dagger into the man's chest. Cale died from his injuries, enraging the citizens of Socorro.

Convicted of murder in District Court on December 8, Fowler was sentenced to hang on January 4, 1884. The hanging did not occur, due to an appeal being filed by Fowler's attorneys, Thomas B. Catron (a member of the Santa Fe Ring) and Neil B. Field. A series of events followed. The militia was called to guard the prisoner's cell in fears the man would be lynched. However, under orders from the governor, the militia was removed on January 20 due to the high expense. Sheriff Pete Simpson also left town, giving the town an opportunity to deliver its own form of justice.

During his time in jail, it was learned by the *Lincoln County Leader*, Fowler and the other prisoners held a mock trial during which one of the other prisoners was arraigned for murder. Fowler played the judge and had the audacity to say to the prisoner (whom they had pretended to convict), "A man who would murder another for a watch and a lot of old clothes was unworthy of mercy." This callous statement shocked the reporting newspaper.

Two hundred armed men surrounded the Socorro jail, demanding the key, which was freely given by the jailer. Joel A. Fowler was then removed from his cell. The *Las Vegas Optic* reported, "Fowler loudly called on Heaven to protect him, when some wag in the crowd called out: 'It's a cold night for angels, Joel. Better call on someone nearer town. You are in the hands of law-abiding citizens, Mr. Fowler, and they will see that you get your just deserts.'"

Fowler was said to be crying and begging for forgiveness on his way to the chosen cottonwood tree, but to no avail. He even begged to be allowed to climb up in the tree and jump out, but instead a noose was tightened around his neck and the deed was completed. To make sure, some of the men pulled down on Fowler's legs to complete the task. Sheriff Pete Simpson reportedly sat down and cried the next morning when he returned to see what had occurred.

# GEORGE MUSGRAVE

As a lesser-known member of the "Black-Jack" Ketchum Gang, George Musgrave kicked up his own dust in the Land of Enchantment. Going by several aliases such as Jeff Davis and Jesse Williams, George and his brothers Colney and Volney participated in horse theft, robbing stagecoaches and trains in eastern Arizona and the New Mexico Territory that resulted in the accumulation of $20,000 to $40,000.

Although he denied his involvement later in life, George Musgrave was said to have joined the "Black-Jack" Ketchum Gang in the fall of 1896 after he was indicted for horse theft in Chaves County. The gang consisted of five members—all were said to have been law-abiding citizens and good cowboys working in the Roswell area until their first heist in the mountain community of Nogal, New Mexico (close to present-day Ruidoso), where the gang held up the bank. The townsfolk resisted, resulting in no rewards for their feeble first attempt.

Even with an obvious criminal record, George Musgrave was also falsely accused of a crime. Marshal Foraker, who brought a prisoner by the name of George Massagee to Albuquerque to face trial, became frustrated at the rumor mill's counterfeit tales.

In a March 10, 1902 article from the *Albuquerque Citizen*, Marshal Creighton Foraker is quoted as talking about the rumors surrounding the arrest of George Musgrave and George Massagee as being false news, and he relayed the story of an incident George Musgrave was guilty of instead:

> *This man Massagee was one of the gangs* [members] *that terrorized eastern New Mexico and so were Wit Neil* [Whit Neal]*, J. Cook and Joe Robertson who were arrested in Arizona, but the leader of the gang was Henry Hawkins. George Musgrave was not the leader, was not a member, was not a bandit and we don't want him….He* [Musgrave] *has not been in New Mexico in six years. I'll stake a thousand dollars on that. How the stories started, unless it was from El Paso, I don't know.*

Foraker referenced the Parker murder by saying:

> *George Musgrave is not wanted. He and a man named Parker were in partnership some eight years ago in cattle stealing. They had a brand of their own and stole calves. It got hot for them, and Parker* [George T.] *suggested to Musgrave that as he was foot loose, he skip out. Parker agreed to buy his interest and pay the money to Musgrave's mother. Then when the storm broke, all blame was to be put on Musgrave. Musgrave agreed and the scheme was carried out except that Parker did not pay the money to Musgrave's mother but put it in his pocket.*

*Musgrave heard of it and sent word to Parker to pay his mother, or he would kill him. Parker told him he would not and one day Musgrave went over to when he was with about twenty-five cattle men. He walked up to Parker and with his left hand he shook Parker's right hand, at the same time shooting and killing Parker with his right hand. No attempt was made to hold or arrest Musgrave, and everyone said Parker got just what he deserved. Musgrave skipped out and has not been back since.*

Musgrave was still accused of murdering George Parker in the New Mexico Territory in October 1896, and another article appeared in the early newspapers. Sheriff Charles L. Ballard from North Platte, Nebraska, was alerted to Musgrave's crime in Omaha through some cowboys who recognized him and turned Musgrave in to authorities. Ballard and Musgrave returned to Roswell, New Mexico, after his capture in January 1910 so the accused could stand trial for the death. Musgrave was reported to be just a boy of sixteen when he committed the crime, and his appearance had changed significantly over the years, as he had matured into a handsome man of twenty-nine with a broad build and tall stature.

Without the eagle eye of Omaha, Nebraska citizens, George Musgrave would have been able to blend in with the population. Musgrave was heard to have commented that he would have been able to avoid capture if he had not made a comment about Parker to a man in Colorado. Rumors and stories began to fly in the streets of Omaha about the circumstances of the Parker murder, but Musgrave told his side of the story to the *Roswell Daily Record* in a rare interview:

*My trouble with Parker started over a trade, in which I sold him cattle for horses, he to pay me the difference in cash. I was then fifteen years old. After the trade it developed that the horses, he traded me were stolen property, and he advised me to leave the country, telling me he would look after my property while I was gone and until it was safe for me to come back. Trouble was brewing over the stolen horses and Parker scared me into leaving because I was in possession of the stolen property.*

*Taking Parker's advice, I left the country. But I returned in a year and a half, deciding to see if there was a charge against me. Upon going to my father's ranch, I learned that Parker had taken practically all of my mother's cattle, even the calves, claiming I had sold them to him for $500, the money I needed to leave the country on. I went at once to* *the round-up where Parker was to see him about it for, I had made no such sale to him. Parker had robbed me in the trade and robbed mother of her stock.*

*When I reached the roundup, Parker was not at the wagon but some of the boys went out and told him to come in, as I was there to see him. As he came into the camp, he moved his belt around so that his gun was in front instead of at the side. When he dismounted, he reached for his gun, and as I heard that he was going to get me if he could, I decided that it was time to be doing something.*

After the killing, Musgrave reportedly rode west to the railroad, turned his horse loose and left the area on the train. When pressed about his connection with the Black-Jack Ketchum Gang, he flat-out denied being involved and said that "all the things of which he was accused are false."

After leaving the New Mexico Territory, Musgrave stated that he spent most of his time in Colorado, Omaha, Kansas City and Chicago, working as a cattle broker. Some other background information given to the reporter included the fact that he had married two years prior to his arrest, that his parents were living east of El Paso, Texas (although he was not too sure exactly where, as he thought it was Isleta), and that he was a member in good standing of the Elks Lodge of Grand Junction, Colorado—just not under the name George Musgrave, as he was using the name "Mason" instead.

The Old West was of great interest to the citizens of the United States, so when a "celebrity" of that era was captured, it was a big deal. George Musgrave was not a fan of this notoriety. The story relayed in the *Roswell Daily Record* states that when Sheriff Ballard and Musgrave were waiting at the Union Station in Denver, Colorado, for a southbound train to Fort Worth/Dallas, a reporter with a "kodak" stepped forward to set up his camera. Just as the plate was being inserted into the camera, Musgrave "swung forward and kicked a hole in the picture machine and breaking it all to pieces."

Musgrave expressed his dismay at being arrested, largely due to the embarrassment it caused his wife. "What little education I have, I have picked up since leaving New Mexico and in the business world. For years I have never carried a firearm or weapon of any kind. I have been living a square, honest life and dealing honestly with all men, in strictly commercial work." Musgrave continued, "I always felt that sometimes I would want this charge against me settled, and cleared away, if possible, but it's coming has been a shock to me on account of my wife."

Harry Aguayo, a La Luz resident and witness to the Parker incident, told a different version of the story in an article in the *Alamogordo Daily News* on August 11, 1957. Aguayo put Musgrave's age as closer to twenty years, and he had a $10,000 reward on his head for his outlaw activities in Arizona. Aguayo reported that Musgrave was in the company of a large man with a full beard and the "meanest grey eyes that I had ever seen"—later identified in a newspaper column by Howard Bryan as Bob Hayes. Both men were in rugged clothes and looked to have been on the trail a long time.

The two weary men asked for some food and water from the roundup cook of the Diamond A Ranch near the Rio Felix in Chaves County, New Mexico, about forty miles southwest of Roswell, which they were gladly given. Musgrave was cordial with the cowboys, as he knew most of them, and began to joke with the group. Aguayo noted that when Musgrave sat down, he used Parker's bedroll as a cushion—it's uncertain if this was on purpose. After their meal, Musgrave and his companion rolled some Bull Durham tobacco and smoked until the men started to drift into camp for dinner. George Parker and Billy Phillips of the Bar V Ranch and Les Harmon rode into camp and went to the water barrel, nodding to Musgrave, not recognizing him.

According to Aguayo, Musgrave jumped up and said, "Hello George" and stuck his hand out to Parker to shake. As Parker went to shake the young man's hand, Musgrave said, "I've come all the way across this territory to kill you and now I am going to do it." Musgrave drew his Colt .45 pistol and shot the clueless man four times. It was then that Musgrave's companion first spoke to the fifteen stunned cowboys. "Stand still boys, I'll kill the first one that moves. The first man to make a flash dies." No one moved since this man was holding a Colt .45.

After the killing, Musgrave took the wranglers to the remuda to pick out his choice of horses. It was pointed out that Musgrave had picked a mean one: "Parker's old Swallow-fork horse with the split ears." The men worried that Musgrave would turn on them if he got injured if the horse bucked him off, but the horse did not put up a fight when ridden away by Musgrave's friend. The camp was stripped of weapons save an old .44 rifle and a few six-guns left behind.

George Parker had been shot at such close range in the chest, each shoulder and head that his shirt caught fire, smoldering while Musgrave chose his livestock. A small fire erupted once the men left. Aguayo and a few of the cowboys put out the flames growing on the victim's chest.

Aguayo's story varies a bit from the *Roswell Daily Record* article in that he has Musgrave being recognized and captured in Montana when Frank Parks of the Bloom Cattle Company saw him and turned him over to the authorities. Aguayo went on to say that Musgrave was from a good family in Texas, and he did not know the real reason he went bad. This information was different from an *Albuquerque Journal* article from July 25, 1907, which stated that Musgrave originally came from a wealthy New Mexico family who experienced a reversal of fortune. George, being the eldest of the sons, took it upon himself to provide for his family—unfortunately, mostly by illegal methods.

When Sheriff Ballard returned to Roswell with his quarry, Musgrave was taken before District Judge William H. Pope for indictment. Musgrave was released on a $10,000 bond pending his trial in May 1910. It is said that the evidence given by District Attorney L.O. Fullen was so convincing that when his trial began in Roswell on May 27, 1910, Judge Pope revoked Musgrave's bond midway through the trial and ordered him to be held in jail.

Musgrave pleaded self-defense (which was the usual plea of this era), which was supported by the testimonies of two cowboy witnesses: Lycurgus L. Johnson and a man who was identified only as "Les Miserables," who stated that George Parker reached for his gun, therefore forcing Musgrave to shoot him in self-defense. The testimony worked, as Musgrave was acquitted and released on June 3, 1910.

Although there are reports that George Musgrave returned to Nebraska to live out a law-abiding life, others contest that his trails led him to South America and to his death in 1947.

## CHARLES KENNEDY

Arriving in New Mexico around 1868 as a gold prospector and miner, Charles Kennedy, sometimes known as Charley Canady, began looking for gold in Humbug Gulch close to Elizabethtown, New Mexico. According to the *Santa Fe Weekly Post* of 1868, he and his two partners from Georgetown and Central came across some old Spanish diggings about twenty miles west of the Rio Grande in Mill's Gulch. As they opened a shaft, they were surprised to discover a skeleton of a man standing upright surrounded by mining tools and the unfortunate person's gold pan.

Their guide, a man known only as La Blanc, told them of a Pueblo Indian legend concerning the Spanish mines. La Blanc told of many Spaniards who were buried alive while working in the mines—the discovery of the skeleton corroborated this story. La Blanc was partnered with Judge Blackwood and Christopher "Kit" Carson in the ownership of this land where the tragic mine was found.

Once the mine played out, Kennedy set up in a small trading post nestled in the picturesque Carson National Forest near Scully Mountain, turning it into a den of horrors for unsuspecting travelers. The bustling mining town of Elizabethtown, with more than seven thousand residents, sometimes did not have enough accommodations for everyone, so they would travel on the road from Mora to Taos a little farther to the Kennedy place. There they would be fed a meal, and their livestock would also be corralled and fed.

Over the course of several years, the Kennedy trading post saw steady business as the gold miners flocked to the region. Everything seemed above board until one frigidly cold night when a Ute woman fell through the door of John Pearson's saloon. Half-frozen and hysterical, the woman scanned the room for help. Fortunately for her, in this saloon were the gentleman gunfighter Clay Allison and his cohort, Davy Crockett (nephew of his famous namesake), trying to keep away the cold with a glass of whiskey.

The men listened in silence as the Native woman relayed an awful story. At the trading post, a recent guest was enjoying his supper when he innocently asked if they had any trouble with Indians in area. To this Kennedy's seven-year-old son spoke up by saying, "Sure, don't you smell the one Papa killed and put under the floor last night?" Enraged, Kennedy grabbed the boy by the hair and slammed the young child's head into the rock fireplace, killing him. The maniacal man then turned his rifle on the inquisitive stranger, killing him instantly as well.

Kennedy's wife, understandably in complete shock, began screaming, causing him to lock her in the bedroom while he proceeded to drink himself into a stupor. Stories state that the woman escaped through a fireplace and walked the distance to the saloon to find help. This would have been an incredible feat since it was, in some accounts, a blinding snowstorm. Allison and a posse of outraged men arrived at the roadside inn to find Kennedy still in a stupor and took the drunken man to Elizabethtown.

In a grand jury inquiry, Jose Cortez, an employee of Kennedy's, was a witness. During Cortez's testimony, he recounted an event that had

ROBERT CLAY ALLISON
1840 — 1887

HE NEVER KILLED A MAN
THAT DID NOT NEED KILLING

As a gunfighter, Clay Allison was only shot once—by his own hand as he attempted to remove mules from Fort Union. *Courtesy author's collection.*

occurred around Christmas 1869 when he was awakened by a gunshot in the middle of the night. When he entered a room lit by candlelight, he saw the body of a large American man with red whiskers on the floor with a bullet wound to the head, obviously deceased. When asked to help bury the body, Cortez refused and immediately went to Taos. He wouldn't tell anyone of the story until this day. The defense attorney attempted to disprove Cortez's story but was unsuccessful. Bones were brought to the courtroom from the crime scene; Drs. Westerling and Bradford were unable to determine if they were human but nonetheless stated that the bones came from a human body, which caused a great deal of confusion with the jury, but they ignored the obvious.

Before actions could begin the next day, a resident of Taos Pueblo came to town to report the discovery of a human skeleton under the floor at

Once boasting seven thousand citizens, Elizabethtown was a booming gold mining hub and home to a serial killer. *Courtesy of author.*

the Kennedy place. Judge McBride proceeded to the scene to complete a coroner's inquest. McBride found a skeleton of what appeared to be a large man with red whiskers. His skull had been shattered, consistent with a gunshot wound. This fact corroborated the testimony given by Jose Cortez the day before.

According to the *Santa Fe New Mexican* in October 1870, a public meeting was held with twenty-five prospective jury members from which twelve men would be chosen by the defendant. Kennedy was given an impromptu trial using the selected jury, but even with the evidence presented and the fact that Kennedy could not account for the missing visitors, a hung grand jury resulted, leading Kennedy to believe, since he had some influence in Elizabethtown, that he would literally get away with murder.

Sheriff Agnes Houx and his officers did not expect any trouble from Kennedy or the town, but the prisoner was housed in a makeshift log cabin that had been reinforced with iron and two guards. At 11:00 p.m. on the seventh of October, a large group of armed and hooded men overtook one of the guards to obtain access to Kennedy. The struggling prisoner was carried to the old slaughterhouse about a half a mile outside town and hanged from a rafter without ceremony.

The body, found the next morning, was the subject of another coroner's jury headed by Judge McBride, who confirmed that Kennedy indeed had died from hanging. In McBride's report, he wrote, "So ended the life of this cold-blooded assassin. No doubt, if the truth were known, the crime which was brought to light, is but one of many he has perpetrated. There is a general feeling of satisfaction that he is at last beyond the power of doing further harm. Still while we have no word of pity for the murderer, we cannot commend the action of those who hung him. The time has passed when it was necessary for people of this community to take the punishment of offenders in their own hands."

Another version of the story was relayed by an article in the *Taos News*, dated January 15, 2005, which has the crowd storming the jail and putting a rope around Kennedy's neck so he could be dragged through town until

Owner of the St. James Hotel Henri Lambert was once a head chef for Presidents Abraham Lincoln and Ulysses S. Grant. *Courtesy of author.*

he died. The famed gunfighter Clay Allison, who had a violent temper, was said to be a part of this group and allegedly decapitated Kennedy and possibly threw the head into a nearby ditch, never to be found again. In her book *Satan's Paradise*, Agnes Morley Cleaveland, a frontier resident of Cimarron, alleged that Allison put the head into a sack, whereupon he took it to Lambert's Inn for display about twenty-six miles away, after which it would eventually be sent to the Smithsonian for study. According to the *Taos News* article, the townsfolk thought it ironic that Allison was the one to cut off Kennedy's head since it was the latter who had rebuked the gunfighter for dancing naked on the bar in Elizabethtown.

Others have written that it was well-known Charles Kennedy was responsible for the murder of at least fourteen American travelers, several Natives who were unlucky enough to cross paths with the murderer and two more of his children before that fateful night. Given these facts, along with the detail that he would regularly beat his wife, the death of possibly New Mexico's first serial killer was not mourned.

## COAL-OIL JOHNNIE AND TOM TAYLOR

An article in the July 15, 1987 edition of the *Santa Fe Reporter* written by historian/author Marc Simmons sheds light on a few desperados who operated in the northern New Mexico Territory in the 1870s.

Around 1872, men known as Coal-Oil Johnnie and Tom Taylor, two low-rank bandits, were terrorizing the stagecoaches that plied the Santa Fe Trail in the New Mexico Territory in the vicinity of Las Vegas. Barlow and Sanderson Company, one of the major stage lines along the trail, lost so many strongboxes to the robbers that it put a large reward on the heads of the thieves to stop the raids. These rewards were topped by the owners of the Maxwell Land Grant Company, who put an additional $2,000 price on each of the outlaw's heads.

These bad men, although not as well known as Billy the Kid or Tom Ketchum, were ruthless in their trade. Newspaper reports tell tales of cunning and outright heartlessness, as they would approach their intended victim along the road and were as courteous and cordial as anyone could ask. They'd ride along with the person for a while to build up trust and then strike without warning. One of the two robbers would make a statement such as, "I'm tired of your company," and then then victim would be shot

Fort Union was the largest military fort in the territory, operating from 1851 to 1891, with three separate building phases, from wood to adobe. *Courtesy of author.*

Known to be highly haunted, the St. James Hotel in Cimarron has hosted names like Annie Oakley, Jesse James and many others. *Courtesy author's collection.*

immediately, according to early accounts. The poor person would then be stripped of their valuables and left as fodder for the coyotes and elements.

Word of the sizable reward spread from the New Mexico Territory to Texas, where two bounty hunters, Frank Stewart and Jim McIntyre, caught wind of the potential rewards and decided to rid their neighbors of the menace. Likely entering New Mexico seven miles from Fort Union at Collier's Soap Factory, the bounty hunters immediately set up an ambush in the nearby volcanic lava fields of the Turkey Mountains, where they heard the outlaws traveled frequently.

Their planning saw results quickly, as the bandits were spotted and brought to justice in a swarm of bullets. According to Simmons, the story in the local papers read, "The victims were shot full of holes and their miserable remains were taken to Cimarron." As was the custom in many towns, the doors to the St. James Hotel in Cimarron were removed and were put into service as makeshift stretchers to hold the two bodies for photographic purposes.

A strange twist to this story involves one of the bounty hunters who remained in the Land of Enchantment for several years after, collecting their bounties, only to eventually become bandits themselves. Karma struck a heavy blow when Jim McIntyre was later killed by the infamous gunfighter Luke Short when he returned to Texas. Frank Stewart's whereabouts were said to be unknown in 1987, but later articles and books have new information that suggests Stewart became a range detective for the Panhandle Stockman's Association/Canadian Cattle Association and would join Pat Garrett, Charlie Siringo, Barney Mason and others in the 1880 pursuit of Billy the Kid through southeastern New Mexico; he was also involved in the Stinking Springs incident.

## George W. "Buffalo Bill" Spawn/ Joseph "Dutch Joe" Hubert/Nicolas Provencia

Not much is known about this small-time horse thief who roamed the southwestern section of the New Mexico Territory, most likely in the company of members of the John Kinney Gang.

One of Spawn's greatest joys was to steal horses and mules from the many territory forts of the U.S. government in the territory. In June 1887, Spawn and his cohort, Nicolas "Nick" Provencia, were captured and jailed in Mesilla by Sheriff Mariano Barela. Housed with another thief, Joseph "Dutch Joe" Hubert, Spawn and Provencia began to devise a plan to gain their release from the jail.

Proving the adage "there's no honor among thieves," the pair of horse thieves told Sheriff Barela that they were told in confidence by Hubert that he boasted about robbing several stagecoaches in Cooke's Canyon, and they had all the details. Robbing stagecoaches was a much bigger crime, so the sheriff took the bait and promised the men their freedom if they would testify against Hubert in the U.S. District Court in Mesilla—

an opportunity Spawn and Provencia gladly jumped on.

Hubert was indicted by a grand jury with the information supplied by Spawn and Provencia, and Dutch Joe was charged with attempting to rob the mails and obstructing passage of the mail in connection with the alleged stagecoach robberies that occurred north of Deming during a sixteen-month timeframe.

The first hold-up where Dutch Joe was accompanied by Roscoe Burrell and another man named Henry came on January 12, 1876, where $4,000 in silver bullion was stolen from a stagecoach containing passengers, cattle baron John Chisum and his attorney, Thomas F. Donway. Chisum was said to have had more than $1,000 in cash on his person but hid it in his boot.

The second was in May 1877 at the same spot as the first, accomplished with the help of Robert "Bob" Martin, but this time their luck was not as good. The four passengers were not rich cattle barons, so the extent of the bounty was $1.50 and a pistol. The owner of the pistol, John B. Morrill, chided the robbers by saying, "You should have known better than to strike such a poor crowd."

Details given by Spawn and Provencia included the location of where the silver bars were buried after the robbery and the fact that Dutch Joe and his pals returned, dug it up and took it to a ranch in Santa Teresa before taking the silver to Chihuahua, Mexico, where it was made into coins.

*Top*: Sheriff Barela had his hands full with the criminal element in the center of the New Mexico Territory. *Courtesy author's collection.*

*Bottom*: As one of the largest cattle ranchers in New Mexico, John Chisum had his fair share of dealing with criminal elements. *Courtesy author's collection.*

During jury selection, one perspective juror was asked if he knew the defendant, to which Hubert interrupted by saying, "If he does, he knows nothing but good of me." After the jury was sworn in, the defendant was asked if he had any objections to the panel, to which he replied, "Yes, I want to get all of the ugly men off of it."

The middle-aged German immigrant chose to defend himself in the trial after dismissing his defense attorney, John Ryan, in the hopes of proving his innocence and illuminating the ridiculousness of the charges. Dramatically shouting at the jury with his thick German accent, Hubert made a point: "It is more honorable to make an example of a thief by shooting him than to enter the jail and hire horse thieves to testify against an honorable man."

In his closing arguments, Hubert was still on a roll:

> *There's George Spawn that big lummox of an American, he testifies against me so he can get clean out of jail. The big American was a soldier ten years and don't know ABC. He makes his living by stealing and robbing. Spawn sleeps with Nick, he is his bosom friend, and as soon as these two thieves get through appearing against me, they will be set free from jail and have a horse and rifle given to them, so they can go into Arizona and steal Apache horses. That's their business. I leave my case to God and you. If you don't think them thieves swore to the truth, you can't find me guilty.*

Unfortunately for Hubert, the jury did find him guilty, and Judge Warren Bristol passed down a sentence of thirteen years of hard labor at the Missouri State Penitentiary and a $200 fine. George Spawn and Nicolas Provencia gained their freedom that day just as Dutch Joe had predicted. Hubert's decision to defend himself backfired since he reportedly "all but admitted" that he committed the crimes during his closing arguments.

Old habits are hard to break. By August of the same year, George "Buffalo Bill" Spawn was back to his old ways and stole two government mules from the Lincoln County, New Mexico Indian agent with another horse thief, Serafin Aragon. Although they were followed to Tularosa, they were not captured—Aragon was later captured in Lincoln. Spawn went to La Luz and laid low for a while before he borrowed a horse and pistol and went to Tularosa, where he traded the horse; then he went on to the next village, where he sold this horse. Spawn eventually left the area in a wagon owned by Antonio Sanchez that was headed for Santa Fe. Eventually, Spawn was arrested at the springs about five miles outside Galisteo by Deputy Sheriff McGentry and Mr. Biernstein.

An article that appeared in the December 25, 1877 edition of the *Weekly New Mexican* stated, "George W. Spawn, alias Buffalo Bill, convicted at the last of U.S. District Court held at Mesilla for stealing government mules from the Mescalero Apache Reservation and sentenced to five years imprisonment in the Missouri State Penitentiary, took his departure for his destination in custody of Marshal Sherman and his deputy, Paul Schwartz."

Commentary in the *Grant County Herald* of Silver City stated about Dutch Joe: "We do not mourn, as Rachel for her first-born, because of Joe's departure, but rather, we rejoice that he is going to a please [*sic*] where his acquisitive disposition will not interfere with the welfare of others. And where the chastening rigor of prison discipline may learn him to respect the law of meum et tuum."

## WILLIAM "WILD BILL" MARTIN/ ROBERT "BOB" NELSON/ JOSE M. "PORTUGUESE JOE" CARROLA (CARROLLS)

Southwestern New Mexico Territory was a haven for outlaws and scoundrels, as it was far enough away from the Texas border near where most of these bandits hailed and close enough to the lawless Arizona Territory just in case things got too rough.

Horse and cattle thieves were abundant in this region since it was easy to place the blame on the resident Apache tribes, who were giving law enforcement and ranchers fits by participating in the same practices. The mountainous areas around the Gila River near the Sycamore Creek junction close to Silver City, New Mexico, sheltered many secret headquarters and rendezvous points for the various gangs of thieves that roamed at liberty.

Led by Robert "Bob" Nelson, a group of three men terrorized ranchers by relieving them of their various livestock. Accompanying Nelson in the operations were William "Wild Bill" Martin, John Donaldson and Jose M. "Portuguese Joe" Carrola (sometimes referred to as Carrolls).

Nelson's neighbor, Captain R.N. Calhoun, who worked for the Perry Ranch, was one of those locals who noticed a horse on Nelson's ranch that was reported stolen in nearby Silver City. When Calhoun confronted Nelson about his suspicions, he was emphatically told to "keep his mouth shut." Shortly after this encounter, Calhoun responded to a disturbance at the Perry Ranch, where he thought Apaches were raiding the horses. As Calhoun entered the doorway to exit the bunkhouse, he was struck down by a rifle shot to the chest.

While doing an investigation the next morning, Frank Venable, another Perry ranch hand, discovered a rifle shell with some distinct markings that he recognized from a Henry rifle that he had sold to Donaciano Dominguez, who later sold the weapon to Wild Bill Martin. These findings were reported to ranch owner John Perry, who immediately rounded up a posse from the surrounding ranches and contacted Sheriff Harvey Whitehill in Silver City.

In an attempt to find Nelson and his gang, Perry sent word to member John Donaldson to come to the ranch house for a meeting, promising the man that he would not be harmed. Donaldson arrived the next night and admitted that one of Perry's horses had been stolen the night Calhoun was shot and promised to have the animal back if Perry would remain quiet about the situation. Donaldson then promised that he and some of the other members of the gang would return to the Perry ranch for further negotiations the next day.

As the four horse thieves slowly rode up to the ranch, they went past the front of the house to line up directly with the front door. Spurring their horses, the men charged the front door and were met with gunfire supplied by Sheriff Whitehill and his posse members. After the smoke cleared, Wild Bill Martin, Portuguese Jose Carrola and John Donaldson lay dead on the blood-soaked ground.

Nelson, although shot in the hip and thigh, was able to retreat, dropping his rifle when shot. He drew his pistol and dropped it as well without firing, as he had to hold his hands over his wounds as he rode away without use of his reins as well. The posse pursued Nelson and found his dropped hat on the trail and then later his dead horse—it had been shot in the gun battle as well.

Somehow Nelson was able to get to a horse from a nearby ranch and ride away, though in great pain from his wounds. The desperado's saddle was found in the surrounding hills about six months later, but Nelson was nowhere to be found. An interesting side note on Nelson concerns a "half-breed" Indian who was hired by Whitehill to track Nelson; he returned to Silver City stating that he was nowhere to be found, but it was also noticed that this tracker was spending money quite generously in the saloons, making people wonder if this was Nelson's money he was being so free with.

## Tom Bowe

According to author/historian Leon Metz, Thomas/Tom Bowe was a man who "reveled in unnecessary violence." This statement was probably true for most of the characters in this book as well, but Bowe had a dark cloud following him.

Entering New Mexico in 1872, Bowe was said to have been fresh from killing a man in Pueblo, Colorado—although unproven, he decided that Santa Fe was more suited to him. This proved to be an incorrect statement, as he was quickly run out of the City Different shortly after for "factious misbehavior." Tom had a tendency of shooting up the gambling houses he frequented, and the Santa Fe citizens did not appreciate this behavior.

From the New Mexico Territory, Bowe traveled west to the Arizona Territory to see what kind of trouble he could stir up there. Suspected of immediately joining a gang of robbers (possibly the High Five Gang), Bowe was thought to have participated in several stagecoach robberies with his companions Hart and Phillips only, although he was never arrested for these crimes. According to the March 20, 1884 article of the *New Mexican Review*, Bowe committed a stage robbery in the winter of 1874 in Arizona during which a man named Sam Bullock was relieved of $1,600. In a retraction printed by the *Arizona Silver Belt* on March 22, 1884, Bullock claimed that he was in Globe, Arizona, at the time of the robbery and was not robbed.

On the run again in late 1874, Tom Bowe drifted from Arizona and showed up in the newspaper articles of Silver City, New Mexico, accompanied by his stage robbing buddies, who were thought to be murderers as well. Ward's Dance Hall soon became a favorite watering hole for the handsome, slim, thirty-year-old with dark hair and moustache who was said to like to skulk around town wearing dark clothing, rarely looking up and wearing his hat low. When Bowe did speak, it was with a slight Irish accent.

An argument over a game of faro the next spring left Bowe's acquaintance Jack Carter dead from a gunshot by Bowe's hand. Jack died on the spot, and a panicked Bowe headed for the nearby mountains to hide out in a lime kiln. Grant County sheriff Harvey Whitehill pulled together a four-man posse to accompany him to find the killer. Bowe was located and brought back to Silver City, where the charges were dropped. Self-defense law ruled the West.

Nothing was written about Tom Bowe after this event until October 5, 1877, when Bowe and one of Silver City's wealthiest citizen's and saloon operators, Richard "Dick" Howlett, entered George Spears's saloon for a friendly game of poker after carousing together most of the week. The poker game included Bowe, Howlett and two of the town's first sheriffs, Richard

Hudson and John Justice. All was going well until Bowe's chip count began to fade away significantly.

During an important hand with a large pot, Howlett called Bowe's bluff and chose a poor time to poke fun at the Irishman's card playing abilities. Howlett was warned by Richard Hudson to steer clear of this action since Bowe did not have a good sense of humor, especially when it came to money. A combination of a large pot, alcohol, ill-timed ridicule and the potential of losing big proved to be too much for Bowe and deadly for Howlett. Bowe's six-shooter ended the game and Howlett's life.

Not making the same mistake as he did a few years prior, Bowe fled to Mexico after he obtained some help with a horse, blankets, food and firearms from friends who lived in the nearby hills. Nothing is written about why Bowe left Mexico for California and then moved across the United States to live in New York City, but it is written by Metz that Bowe eventually grew "tired of life in the metropolis" and went west again—this time to Montana, where he assumed the name Pat Delaney.

Rewards for Bowe's arrest were substantial given the prominence of Howlett. The Territory of New Mexico offered $500, the citizens of Silver City put in $450, the Howlett estate presented $500 and the brother of the deceased, Charles Howlett, pitched in $200 to make the total reward $1,650.

Seven years after the death of Richard Howlett, Detective Edward Connors of Lordsburg, New Mexico, was able to arrest and extradite Bowe from Montana to the New Mexico Territory by order of the governor of New Mexico, where the murder case was eventually dropped.

# JAMES ALLEN

As a tall, slender young man of about twenty-three, James Allen came to east Las Vegas, New Mexico, in August 1879 from Leadville, Colorado, where he had lived for four years, according to the March 4, 1880 edition of the *Las Vegas Daily Gazette*. In one of the roughest towns of the Wild West, Allen gained employment as a waiter at the St. Nicolas Hotel. This job would change his life forever.

James A. Morehead, traveling wholesale liquor agent for the firm of Derby & Derby and a "gentleman of an excellent family…from St. Louis where his aged parents now live," arrived at the dining room of the hotel late on the morning of March 1, 1880, and requested a breakfast of fried eggs.

For reasons unknown, Allen took offense to the request, stating rudely that the cook was too busy to prepare the meal. The matter was dropped that morning, but the next morning, Morehead, described as a large, robust man of between thirty-five and forty years of age, was said to have jokingly referred to the previous morning, adding that "it would not be long until the cook would not have time to fry stake [*sic*]."

This remark incensed Allen, but Morehead had already grabbed Allen by the arm and thrown him to the floor after Allen took

As the St. Nicholas Hotel in Las Vegas advertised, it "will be kept as a first-class hotel, providing good table, attention and fine wines." *Courtesy author's collection.*

offense. Not satisfied with hand-to-hand combat, James Allen returned to the kitchen to grab his six-shooter to finish the argument. Allen returned to the room with the weapon, called Morehead a son of a b----- and ordered him to get down on his knees. Morehead refused and took a swipe at Allen as he shot, attempting to knock the weapon out of the younger man's hands. The six-shooter discharged; Morehead was hit.

A Black porter was also present and made a move to separate the men, but Allen threatened to shoot him as well. Allen was arrested shortly after the incident as he continued to quietly prepare for the dinner rush. Morehead passed away from his gunshot injury to the liver and stomach between ten and eleven o'clock that evening, despite the best efforts of the local doctors. The *Santa Fe New Mexican* excitedly reported that rumors were flying around Las Vegas that Allen would be lynched that night, but these proved to be false.

Taken to the Las Vegas jail, Allen claimed self-defense and noted that he did not have any intention of killing Morehead. He claimed that he came from a respectable family, which included his parents, a sister and a stepbrother and sister, but he refused to state where he was born since he did not want them to learn of his plight, bringing shame on them.

Allen admitted that he was quick tempered and had a tendency to say things he probably should not, but he was not a violent man. While in he was his jail cell, the paper also reported that Allen complained about the "[f]ilthy conditions and the grub set up was not as good as the article furnished at the ordinary boarding house." The prisoner was also noted to

One of the original jails in Las Vegas now houses a fine arts studio, which still contains the jail cell. *Courtesy author's collection.*

look "worked up to a high state of nervous excitement over the crime and has a generally distressed appearance."

Justice O'Neil held an inquest on the body, and the jury held that Mr. Morehead was killed by James Allen in a "wilful [*sic*] and malicious murder, committed without cause or provocation." James Allen was found guilty of murder in the first degree on August 4, 1880, by a jury in Santa Fe, New Mexico. A motion for a new trial and arrest of judgement was made by Allen's attorney due to the "[i]ndictment upon which he was tried was insufficient, owing to several misapplied terms and technicalities. One of these errors consisted of the use of the word 'affect' instead of 'effect' in a sentence which showed the shooting was committed with the intention to affect the death of the deceased," according to the August 9, 1880 edition of the *Weekly New Mexican*. The court denied the motions. Allen was reported to be expressionless when his sentence was read.

The *Las Vegas Daily Gazette* published a letter written by James Allen to the newspaper on October 17, 1880:

> *Gentlemen:*
> *You were very kind to me when I was a free man, and that is the reason I write this letter asking you to do an act of charity and send me something*

*to protect me from the cold, if it is nothing but a pair of socks. I have no friends or money, and have appealed to them in charge, but have received nothing from them. I may not have long to live but would like to be protected from the cold blast of winter while alive. To be imprisoned and chained is hard but with proper clothing I could bear it very well, if you see fit to send me anything, any of the hack drivers will bring it to jail. Hoping gentlemen, that you will help me, I remain very truly, Yours, James Allen*

While being held in jail with George Davidson, William Mullen (a train robber) and a man known only as De Ochoa, in November 1880, a jailbreak was perpetrated by the three prisoners by the use of wires to pick the lock. Witness William Mullen stated that they traveled from Las Vegas to seven miles northeast of Chaperito on the night of November 11, 1880, where they made camp. As they were almost asleep, the camp was set on by a posse. Although De Ochoa could speak only Spanish, he attempted to rouse his companions, and during the chaos, James Allen and George Davidson were killed.

The coroner's jury concluded that Allen and Davidson, according to the November 16, 1880 edition of the *Las Vegas Daily Gazette*, "died from pistol shot wounds inflicted as shown on examination, by pistols in the hands of Desidero Apodaca and Francisco Martinez, two men deputized for the purpose of taking the prisoners who made their escape from the jail and who were ordered to take them alive, or execute on them any other way, and that they fired on them killing them."

## Joe Stinson

Born in Maine in 1820, Joe Stinson moved west to become a saloon owner in the gold mining town of Elizabethtown in the northern New Mexico Territory around 1879. He then moved on to Santa Fe in 1881. The June 9, 1903 edition of the *Albuquerque Citizen* carried a story that stated that Joseph "Joe" Stinson "abandoned the Atlantic seaboard early and came west to rough it, and rough it hard."

Joe was known to be a good man, except when he was full of liquor. He went from being good old Joe to right bad old Joe. Elizabethtown had a reputation in the 1870s as a place where a man's life was "worth whatever you could get for it, and it was always on sale."

According to a story by old-timer William "Billy" H. Baker, Joe Stinson was not in the mood in 1879 when Wally Henderson came to town. Baker described Henderson as "a mysterious, quiet, drinking sort of cuss, tall, black mustached and gentle in his manner. But his reputation came along with him and the wildest of the boys went slow with him for it was known that he would shoot, and it also leaked out that he was a marksman for whence, who had laid out several pretty confident fellows."

Henderson entered Stinson's saloon and immediately took over, even though Joe was dealing faro a few tables away. Wally began to give everything from the shelves away and, in a drunken move, demanded that they close the saloon at gunpoint. Joe then nodded to Baker to turn out the lights as he put away the faro cards and told the rest of the patrons that the bar was closed for the night. As everyone was leaving, Wally called out to Joe, "I'll kill you some time." To which Joe replied, "All right, but don't let me catch you at it, Wally."

Joe's cool manner worried Baker, who believed that there would be someone to bury before morning by the way he was acting. Unable to sleep, Billy Baker went down to the saloon to sweep up when Joe walked in as well. Anticipating a fight, Joe had returned. When questioned, Joe stated that he had a feeling Wally would return early, and as soon as he spoke those words, the gunman walked into the saloon.

Wally entered, demanding a drink immediately, but when he saw Joe Stinson standing there as well, he felt for his weapon. This move prompted Joe to shoot, letting three shots fly before Wally could even finish his search. The gunman lay dead on the floor. Baker stated that Joe was very calm when he said, "It's a pity, but one of us had to live."

Stinson moved to Santa Fe after this event to open a saloon and gambling house on San Francisco Street near the Plaza and directly opposite of the Claire Hotel, which was considered a first-class establishment. There Joe became acquainted with some of the roughest men Santa Fe had to offer. When Joe's luck ran out, his health failed him, and he was sent to live out the rest of his days in an old soldiers' home in Santa Monica, California, where he is buried.

# JAP CLARK

The name Jasper "Jap" Clark begins to show up in the newspapers around 1905 for various crimes, including the April 4, 1905 murder of former deputy sheriff James M. Chase, who was shot and killed near Estancia, New Mexico, a desolate town nearly dead center in the state.

Testimony of the trial of Jap Clark was covered in the *Albuquerque Journal* of April 13, 1905; the main discussion was who fired the first shot. Deputy Chase was reported to be a dead shot, so according to one witness, if Chase fired the first shot and it was not fatal to Clark, then he was "retreating and fired while moving." After this first initial shot, Clark returned fire, hitting Chase just above the hip, through the abdomen and through the groin. While witnesses debated on who fired first, they all agreed that the incident happened with the "lightning rapidity of the fabled gunfighters of the West."

Attorney General George Washington Prichard, who apparently valued his legal advice as being worth $50,000, testified for the defense. This testimony raised questions and was addressed in the August 6, 1907 article of the *Albuquerque Morning Journal* as a violation of the compiled laws of 1897: "Section 2582. If the solicitor general or any district attorney shall consult with any accused, defend or in any manner shall aid in the defense of any person accused of any crime or misdemeanor in this territory, he shall be fined in any sum not less than five hundred dollars and shall be removed from office by the judgment of the court on such conviction and sentence." The implication was that a man with a $50,000 reputation should know all the law. This caused a stir, especially adding the fact that Jap Clark was a star witness for Mr. Pritchard against the former superintendent of the penitentiary—therefore, they speculated, Pritchard returned the favor.

James Chase had enlisted the help of J.C. (Charley) Gilbert and two men who were known to be determined to drive Clark out of Estancia. When Clark caught wind of the plans, he reportedly "administered a severe beating to Gilbert." Gilbert's response was to write a letter to the El Paso, Texas chief of police, Captain Greet, in which Gilbert relayed the events and his concerns that Jap Clark and W.A. McKean were in Colorado for the expressed purpose of killing him and James Chase.

Gilbert gave his account of the fatal gunfight that ensued between the four men:

> *They tried to shoot me first but were prevented by bystanders. Chase and I were over to the depot when they found him and began to pick a racket. He told them he did not want to fight, and they followed him about two hundred yards when Clark shot at him. He* [Chase] *then began shooting*

*and they both emptied their six shooters. McKean was holding a man with his gun to keep him from helping Chase, or, rather, prevent him from doing anything. After the pistols were shot empty Clark and McKean ran to a saloon nearby and got their 30-40 rifles and began shooting at Chase. When about the third or fourth shot had been fired Chase fell. He died in twenty minutes after he was shot. After the shooting the two men got into a buckboard buggy and as they drove off, I fired five shots at them but did not know that I hit them. I was using a 30-40 U.S. Information has reached here that Clark was shot in the right thigh and was bleeding to death. The shooting grew out of the fact that Chase and I were witnesses in felony cases against both men. The cases were to come up at the next term of court.*

Clark had been previously convicted of horse theft in 1904 but was released on a $3,000 bond pending appeal to the Supreme Court. The court confirmed the sentence, and Clark became a fugitive from justice—therefore allowing him the opportunity to kill Deputy Chase. Many resident ranchers were up in arms about Clark being released in the first place given his criminal tendencies. According to the *Las Vegas Daily Gazette*, "He had been concerned in several shooting scrapes and it

Estancia, which means "resting place," is called the "Heart of New Mexico" since it is the almost dead center of the state. *Courtesy author's collection.*

was known that he threatened with death the man who testified against him at the trial. His quarrel with Chase and Gilbert was caused by his desire to get even with them for their testimony against him."

The *Roswell Daily Record* carried a different account of the trial, stating that Jap Clark claimed self-defense and noted that Chase had threatened to shoot him on sight; Clark was in an ugly mood when they met in Torrance County, it was said. Clark, working for the El Capitan Land and Cattle Company at the time of the incident, had been sent into town for supplies when he encountered Chase. Jap stated that Chase had drawn his pistol on him twice before the fatal shooting occurred. Clark also recounted that during the melee, Chase shot him in the knee. Then, and only then, did Clark return fire, according to his testimony.

After a thirty-six-hour deliberation, Jap Clark was found guilty in the killing of James M. Chase. Clark was no stranger to controversy in his lifetime, as he was well known in the area, having worked for the Block Cattle Company as a cowboy. During this time, Jap narrowly escaped death as the result of being shot three times with a Winchester rifle over a dispute about horse ownership at the village of Picacho in Lincoln County.

In the January 14, 1909 edition of the *Albuquerque Morning Journal*, it was reported the "supreme court affirmed the decision of the lower court by which Jap Clark is sentenced to seven years in the territorial penitentiary, for the killing of Sheriff Chase at Torrance in 1906." The case was extended due to the arguments of Clark's attorney, A.B. Renehan, who pointed out that there was an error since the trial of the case against Clark was held in Estancia, which was not a legally constituted county seat of Torrance County. The county seat was established in 1903 at Progresso and changed in 1905 to Estancia—Renehan argued that this was in violation of the Springer act, which prohibited territorial legislatures from changing county seats. Clark had not been tried at Progresso, and Estancia was not the correct county seat. Although the court took Renehan's points into consideration, the case was tried on the general evidence of the case with great interest in the county seat issue. Clark was convicted, but his partner was acquitted in the case.

# NOT JUST A BOYS' CLUB

When thinking of New Mexico scoundrels, your mind most often veers toward the male variety of troublemakers, but in this beautiful land, women could also be found kicking up dust.

## BELLE LA MONT FOWLER

Some of the West's most interesting characters are women, and this is especially true of Belle Fowler, known as Belle La Mont when she arrived in New Mexico and began work in a saloon/dance hall in Las Vegas. This is where she met and married one of the most dangerous men in the territory, as her skills as a monte and faro dealer caught his eye as much as her beauty.

Born May Belle La Mont (or Lamont), Belle was described in the newspapers as being a striking woman with long dark hair, nearly black eyes and a slight cleft chin; she was tiny at only five-foot-two, but she packed a big punch. This spitfire had been traveling from Oklahoma and Texas as an actress before settling in Las Vegas.

Belle La Mont and Joel Fowler were married in the Santa Fe home of another notorious woman, Monte Verde (Belle Siddons), a Confederate spy, gambler and saloon owner. As the wife of Joel Fowler, Belle had no trouble keeping up with his antics and in most circles was well liked, unlike her husband, who was said to be the most hated man in the territory. Belle was able to ride and shoot as well as anyone, and she was respected for her abilities.

The *Butte Miner*, dated April 7, 1895, ran a story about Joel and Belle Fowler that described her well: "Belle Fowler, the petite, black-eyed siren, once of the variety stage, who figured so sensationally in the New Mexico cities in the eighties [1880s]. He had married her in Santa Fe, and she lived with him during his stay at the ranch. Their matrimonial life was not wholly rose strewn, for she carried upon her cheek as a memento of one episode… it a deep though not disfiguring scar which was currently credited to her husband's knocking her down with a blow from a carbine." One can imagine that this did not set well with the feisty actress.

Belle was said to have worked the ranch with her husband, so she may or may not have been involved in the cattle gathering operations Joel had running in Socorro County. Fowler was a volatile man with violent mood swings, as noted, especially when alcohol was involved. After the sale of his ranch, for an amount that ranged from $50,000 to $100,000, Joel decided to paint the town red. He became exceedingly drunk and killed an upstanding citizen and friend of his during the Good Samaritan's attempt to disarm the rancher.

Fowler's horrible temper and antics had driven the town of Socorro to a breaking point—and this incident was it. Arrested, the rancher was placed in jail, but because of his recent wealthy situation, he was able to hire the best attorneys, infuriating the townsfolk. Fowler "promised that if he got a trial by jury and was convicted, he should make no appeal, but would submit to the death penalty." Joel was tried the next day, convicted and sentenced to hang in thirty days. The look on Fowler's face made everyone realize that this man had no intention of honoring his promise.

In the *Sierra County Advocate* of September 10, 1897, an article stated that Belle rode thirty miles from their ranch each morning for twenty-nine days only to be turned away by the guards. Each time the guards were privy to "her ravings," which were "something awful, but she finally rode away, vowing vengeance on the whole town and asserting that Joe would never hang."

On the afternoon of the twenty-ninth day, Joel caused terror in Socorro as he applied for a new trial, breaking his promise. This would mean a change of venue and a possible acquittal, which happened all too often during this era. Joel had killed in cold blood and delight more than twenty men before he ended the life of his friend John Cole (or Cale) in the Monarch Saloon for making the mistake of interceding during one of Fowler's "ugly drunk" episodes. The town was fed up with living in fear. The knowledge that Belle had sent a summons to some of her husband's most notorious friends—Ben Thompson, Curly Bill, Texas Ed and some of the Earps—to rescue her husband from the gallows, due to arrive by rail a little after midnight, also terrified the town.

Ben Thompson and the rest of the outlaws stepped off the train expecting no resistance but instead were met by at least twenty guns ready to shoot, held by a group soon known as the Socorro Vigilantes. The gang was turned around after they were told that they were not wanted in town and that it would be best to get back on the train. Once the gunmen returned to the train, the conductor was ordered not to stop "inside sixty miles." Not a word was spoken among the Socorro Vigilantes as the train left the station, and then they made their way to the jail.

Joel Fowler was chained to a rock inside the jail cellar. As the vigilantes approached, Fowler was said to be in a cheerful mood, but that was soon to change. In several accounts, Joel was reported to cry murder as he was being led to the cottonwood tree on McCutchen Street on the bitterly cold night in April 1884, begging to be shot rather than "strangled," as he put it. As Fowler prayed for the angels to save him, a man in the group stated, "It's a mighty cold night for angels." In the *Sierra County Advocate* article, Joel was resigned to his fate. When a man called out for him to say his prayers, Joel responded with his last words: "Prayers? I can't think of any at present. Life has been too busy. Well, boys, I thank you all. Joe Fowler never feared anything in heaven or hell. I'm ready, gentlemen." This article also reads that Belle Fowler "had ridden at breakneck speed to the prison, found the body of her husband. One look was all she gave. Turning her horse around she rode away, and Socorro never saw her again."

As an actress known as May Belle Fowler, the Wild West widow drew high acclaim from the newspapers throughout the country. *Courtesy author's collection.*

This statement, though dramatic, proved to be not entirely true, as Belle was seen in Socorro for about one year after Joel's death. Frequenting the dress shops in and around Socorro, she cut quite a pretty image in town. The *Butte Miner* of April 7, 1895, continued with its accounts of Belle after Joel's death. "After his death she came in for a share of his property which was considerable [he had just sold his ranch for $50,000 on the day of the murder], and while it lasted, she was famous among the gambling saloons of Santa Fe, Las Vegas and other New Mexico towns as a player for high stakes, and sometimes as a dealer at faro."

An odd twist to this story has it that Belle and Joel Fowler's ex-wife, Josie (who might also have been a female boxer), toured the gambling halls together. They had become great friends—most likely without Joel's knowledge. Joel's body was conveyed to Texas for burial by Belle. Many accounts had Belle and Josie (who was reported in the papers as Belle's sister) making quick work of the outlaw's money as they traveled from New Mexico to Montana and back.

By 1907, Belle Fowler had become known as May Belle Fowler and had her own stage troupe, starring in plays with Charles Mansville such as *Lost Paradise*, *The Village School Master*, *The Circus Girl* and *Why Girls Leave Home* to rave reviews. Belle's career spanned until 1916 in the newspapers, when she was lost to history.

## Cherokee Dora/Chiquita Cora/Cora the Cowgirl

If ever there was a representative for the phrase "rootin' tootin' cowgirl," it was Cherokee Dora, who was also known as Chiquita Cora or Cora the Cowgirl. She was touted as "'Dare-Devil Girl' who could outshoot, outride and outwit at every turn of work or sport the cleverest of them all." Reported to have been born and raised in the Indian Territory of what is now the state of Oklahoma, Dora did not have an easy childhood, when she was known as Dora French.

The Cherokee Strip, where Dora was born, is a rough section of land where the young girl had to learn tough lessons and skills to survive beginning at the age of seven. She was reported to have murdered her stepfather at seventeen because he allegedly annoyed her when she was in a bad mood; she then fled to the Texas Panhandle. Seems to me that there may be more to this story.

The *Portsmouth Star* from Virginia ran an article in its March 12, 1902 edition that credited Cherokee Dora as "the best pistol shot and most mischievous, proficient and altogether fascinating cowpuncher that ever pulled a Derringer or threw a lariat." The young woman's antics were great fodder for the newspapers, which seemed fascinated by the wild woman, who was also thought to be a train robber.

Cherokee Cora was known by many names. She was also one of the best horsewomen in the western part of the country. *Courtesy author's collection.*

Several newspaper articles mention Dora as being an expert chicken puller. Not familiar with the term, I researched it and found that it was a popular western pastime that was rather cruel in nature. In this "game," a chicken is buried alive with only its neck and head poking out of the ground. A rider would then race past the chicken at full speed and attempt to pull the chicken out of the ground while remaining mounted. Apparently, this was a highly prized skill, and Dora was an expert.

With Dora's intimate knowledge of the bandits who roamed the New Mexico Territory, lawmen attempted to coerce her to help track them down—an offer she always firmly rejected. Cherokee Dora and gambler/well-known card sharp Poker Paul were soon owners of a saloon and gambling house at the "famous Rag Town, on the Rock Island Road." It seemed odd that Dora always had large amounts of cash, "a financial amount far beyond that of any source apparently at her command…this has led to suspicion that Cora Chiquita may be the shrewd advance and investigating agent of a bandit organization proposing bank and train robbery."

In the March 26, 1902 edition of the *Morning Call* from Paterson, New Jersey, it was reported that the partnership with Poker Paul was amiable until "she became jealous of a pretty Mexican girl, upon which La Chiquita promptly shot Paul and scratched the woman until she looked as if she had been in close and energetic communion with a first-class barbed wire fence. Cora then mounted her horse and rode to Santa Rosa."

Dora's reputation grew, as "there was hardly an unmarried man in all that territory [New Mexico] that has not felt the fascination of Dora's charms, and there is not a man married or single, that is not thoroughly afraid of her." Even law enforcement was leery of her since Dora's favorite activity after drinking heavily was to ride full force through the small town of Santa Rosa, New Mexico, with gun blazing to wake everyone up. There was not a sign or lamppost safe from her revolvers. Another fun activity was called the "Dance of the Tenderfoot," where Dora would terrorize unsuspecting easterners by shooting at their feet, demanding they dance.

According to the March 4, 1902 *Anniston Star*:

*Cora Chiquita* [as she was known as well] *is now twenty-three years of age, is slight inform and yet robust and agile and carries a handsome and haughty head crowned heavily with black hair. Her face is lighted with flashing black eyes and teeth of a dazzling white, and she presents a pretty picture in the extreme done is deepest olive. She dresses in nattiest frontier male attire, wears a beplumed [sic] and bespangled sombrero, carries a brace of revolvers at her trim waist and a repeating carbine in her shapely and supple hand. When under the influence of drink, Cora is a warm proposition.*

The paper was quick to add, "As the mood takes her, [Cora is] a good-natured, gentle-hearted and hand-helping woman."

After one episode of becoming drunk and disorderly during which the cowgirl rode her horse into the saloon and set up a round for everyone, a heavily inebriated Dora was arrested and fined. No sooner had she been released than Dora mounted her horse, raced to her tent at the outskirts of town and returned quickly to resume shooting up the town for about two hours, as the townsfolk took cover. The *Minneapolis Journal* recounted Dora's activities in its March 14, 1902 edition, stating, "Cora's shooting was so accurate that the sheriff and his force rested in a basement during her activity."

Dora and a companion were arrested again by a brave marshal who faced her revolvers and placed them in jail without bail. No sooner had the doors shut on Dora's cell than a plan was executed with a use of a saw on the bars for her release. No word on where the saw was obtained. Once she was free, Dora released her companion as well, and both were gone by dawn. Even though a posse was formed, the escapees were not recovered.

During their escape, stories were heard of Dora happening upon a group of railroad construction workers who were less than respectful. This mistake resulted in Dora "reining her horse to its haunches and the leader was covered by her Derringer. Obeying

Newspapers loved the feisty cowgirl they dubbed "Cherokee Cora" or "Cherokee Dora."

a sharp command, he dropped to his knees, and he was only released after a short impromptu prayer and some particularly abject apologies dictated by Dora."

"Cora did not leave her address when she left Santa Rosa, but a friend of Dick Hamilton, who accompanied her, says that Arizona was her destination." No indication has been found as to the validity of this claim, made by the *Tucson Citizen*.

## KATE STEWART/BRONCHO KATE RICHARDSON/ FREEMAN RICHARDSON/JOSEPH AND JULIA SOUZIER

The early 1890s were an explosive time for Silver City madam Kate W. Stewart. Quite literally, for during this time, an attempt was made to blow up the ladies' establishment with what was called "giant powder," according to the *Southwest Sentinel* of October 3, 1893. The *Sierra County Advocate* described the plot: "A dastardly attempt to blow up Miss Kate Stewart's premises was made Thursday evening. About eight o'clock an explosion which jarred upon the sensitive nerves of our citizens was heard, upon investigation it was discovered that a giant powder cartridge had been exploded in a sub-cellar used by the occupants of the house as a wood shed." This attempt followed a break-in in August of the same year when "some light-fingered party obtained considerable plunder."

Kate established her enterprise by opening a business behind the Centennial Saloon and Billiard Hall, lasting until the summer of 1916, when the block was demolished to allow for Abraham Brothers to develop its business block. Kate's house on Bullard in Silver City was described as a pleasure palace, but the house started off as a minimal operation. Kate set up her business in a two-story white clapboard house, but it had secondhand furniture, not the sort of ambiance the madam wanted to establish. Once business began to boom with the gold, silver and copper mining in the area, the ratty furniture was replaced with expensive pieces freighted in from the East Coast.

In April 1895, an inmate of Kate Stewart's house, Mrs. Kate Richardson—better known as "Bronco Kate" or sometimes "Broncho Kate"—passed away in the residence. It was determined that Richardson had been drinking heavily for some time and "concluded to shuffle off this mortal coil," taking a large amount of morphine.

Kate Richardson was the wife of Freeman Richardson, a convicted counterfeiter from Las Cruces, New Mexico, who had been sent to the state penitentiary one year before. Charges had also been levied against Kate and her sister, Mary, during the case, as well another couple, Joseph Souzier and his wife, and William Richardson, possible brother of Freeman, but only the men were given prison sentences for counterfeiting and passing coin. The *Santa Fe New Mexican* stated on September 18, 1893, "The women, very comely and interesting individuals, by the way, were acquitted."

According to an article in the September 25 edition of the *Santa Fe New Mexican*, while the women were being held in the Doña Ana County Courthouse, Joseph Souzier "sent a paper to the women and enclosed in its folds was a letter giving them explicit instructions as to how they should testify. This letter was intercepted by the authorities and was the chief instrument used at the trial in bringing about the conviction of the men."

It is thought, because of her husband's conviction, that the reason behind her entrance into the "world's oldest profession" was to support herself and possibly her sister, Mary.

One year before Kate's death, Freeman served as a trusty for the prison—in fact, Superintendent Bergman valued him "so implicitly that he often sent him to the city with small sums of money to make purchases and the man always proved faithful." This trust was shattered in March 1984 when Freeman and another trusty, Pablo Vigil, were tasked with hauling loads of sand from a nearby arroyo to the prison.

Newly released inmate W.B. Fisher reportedly jumped on the wagon and took over charge of the operation. Vigil testified that he was forced to comply with Fisher and Richardson at gunpoint. Fisher and Richardson jumped off the wagon and instructed Vigil to return home slowly, which he did. The alarm was given, and the superintendent set out the bloodhounds on the convicts' trail while issuing a warrant for the arrest of W.B. Fisher as well. Fisher was captured in April 1894, and Richardson was recaptured some time later.

In a notice run by the *White Oaks Eagle* in February 1896, Julia Francis Souzier filed for divorce from her husband, Joseph, on the grounds of abandonment and cruel treatment; nothing else was found about Julia after this action.

NEW MEXICO CERTAINLY HAD its fill of colorful characters roaming the lands in its formative years. One thing is for certain: you had to be tough to survive the Land of Enchantment. The "scoundrels" in these pages are just a few of the wild men and women who stirred up dust and trouble in the Old West. Some, like Billy the Kid, are still inspiring debates and controversy—proof that legends never die.

# BIBLIOGRAPHY

Alexander, Bob. *Bad Company and Burnt Powder: Justice and Injustice in the Old Southwest*. Denton: University of North Texas Press, 2014.

———. *Lawmen, Outlaws and SOBs*. Vol. 11, *Gunfighters of the Old Southwest*. Silver City, NM: High-Lonesome Books, 2007.

———. *Six-Guns and Single-Jacks: A History of Silver City and Southwest New Mexico*. Silver City, NM: High-Lonesome Books, 2005.

Allison, Clay. *The Life and Death of a Gunfighter: Book One, Part One, The Saga of Clay Allison, Gentleman Gunfighter*. Bloomington, IN: First Books Library, 2002.

Baca, Manuel Cabeza de, and Dolores Gutierrez Mills, et al. *Vicente Silva and His Forty Bandits, His Crimes and Retributions: New Translation from the Spanish*. Santa Fe, NM: Sunstone Press, 2022.

Birchell, Donna Blake. *Tall Tales and Half Truths of Clay Allison*. Charleston, SC: The History Press, 2023.

———. *Wicked Women of New Mexico*. Charleston, SC: The History Press, 2012.

Bryan, Howard. *Incredible Elfego Baca: Good Man, Bad Man of the Old West*. Santa Fe, NM: Clear Light Publishing Company, 1994.

———. *Robbers, Rogues, and Ruffians: True Tales of the Wild West in New Mexico*. Santa Fe, NM: Clear Light Publishing Company, 1991.

———. *True Tales of the American Southwest: Pioneer Recollections of Frontier Adventures*. Santa Fe, NM: Clear Light Publishing Company, 1996.

———. *Wildest of the Wild West: True Tales of a Frontier Town on the Santa Fe Trail.* Santa Fe, NM: Clear Light Publishing Company, 1988.

Burton, Jeff. *Dynamite and Six-Shooter: The Story of Thomas E. "Black Jack" Ketchum.* Santa Fe, NM: Palomino Press, 1970.

Clifford, Frank. *Deep Trails in the Old West: A Frontier Memoir.* Norman: University of Oklahoma Press, 2011.

Crocchiola, Father Stanley Francis. *Desperados of New Mexico.* Santa Fe, NM: Sunstone Press, 2015.

DeArment, Robert. *Deadly Dozen: Twelve Forgotten Gunfighters of the Old West.* Norman: University of Oklahoma Press, 2012.

Groves, Melody. *When Outlaws Wore Badges.* Gilford, CT: TwoDot, 2021.

Hendricks, George. *The Bad Man of the West.* San Antonio, TX: Naylor Company, 1970.

Kelcher, William A. *The Fabulous Frontier: Twelve New Mexico Items.* Santa Fe, NM: Rydal Press, 1946.

———. *The Maxwell Land Grant.* Albuquerque: University of New Mexico Press, 1983.

Lacy, Ann, and Anne Valley-Fox, comps. and eds. *Outlaws & Desperados: A New Mexico Federal Writer's Project Book.* Santa Fe, NM: Sunstone Press, 2008.

L'Aloge, Bob. *Knights of the Sixgun: A Diary of Gunfighters, Outlaws, and Villains of New Mexico.* Las Cruces, NM: Yucca Tree Press, 1991.

———. *Mystery, Mayhem, and Madness in Territorial New Mexico.* Las Cruces, NM: Yucca Tree Press, 1990.

———. *Riders Along the Rio Grande: A Collection of Outlaws, Prostitutes and Vigilantes.* Las Cruces, NM: Yucca Tree Press 1992.

LeMay, John. *Tall Tales and Half Truths of Billy the Kid.* Charleston, SC: The History Press, 2015.

———. *Tall Tales and Half Truths of Pat Garrett.* Charleston, SC: The History Press, 2016.

Lowe, Sam. *Speaking Ill of the Dead: Jerks in New Mexico History.* Gilford, CT: Globe Pequot, 2012.

Maddox, Michael R. *Porter and Ike Stockton: Colorado and New Mexico Border Outlaws.* United States, 2014.

Marriott, Barbara. *Outlaw Tales of New Mexico: True Stories of the Land of Enchantment's Most Infamous Crooks, Culprits and Cutthroats.* Gilford, CT: TwoDot, 2014.

McCown, Dennis. *The Goddess of War: A True Story of Passion, Betrayal and Murder in the Old West.* Santa Fe, NM: Sunstone Press, 2012.

Metz, Leon Claire. *The Encyclopedia of Lawmen, Outlaws, and Gunfighters*. New York: Checkmark Books, 2002.

————. *John Wesley Hardin, Dark Angel of Texas*. Norman: University of Oklahoma Press, 1996.

Parsons, Chuck. *Clay Allison, Portrait of a Shootist*. Pecos, TX: Pioneer Books, 1983.

Rasch, Philip J. *Gunsmoke in Lincoln County*. Goodyear, AZ: Western Publishing Company, 1997.

Rippel, Ellen S. *Outlaws & Outcasts: The Lost Cemetery of Las Vegas, New Mexico*. Las Vegas, NM: East Salt River Press, 2013.

Sonnichsen, C.L. *Tularosa: Last of the Frontier West*. Albuquerque: University of New Mexico Press, 1980.

Thomas, David G. *"Dirty Dave" Rudabaugh, Billy the Kid's Most Feared Companion*. Las Cruces, NM: Doc 45 Publishing, 2023.

Wilson, John P. *Pat Garrett and Billy the Kid: Reminiscences of John P. Meadows*. Albuquerque: University of New Mexico Press, 2004.

# INDEX

# ABOUT THE AUTHOR

Exploring her home state of New Mexico is author Donna Blake Birchell's favorite pastime. Sharing what she has found gives her great joy, and she hopes that you will find as much enjoyment in your own treks of discovery in the Land of Enchantment.